THE UNTOLD HISTORY OF CAPITALISM: PRIMITIVE ACCUMULATION AND THE ANTI-SLAVERY REVOLUTION

THE UNTOLD HISTORY OF CAPITALISM: PRIMITIVE ACCUMULATION AND THE ANTI-SLAVERY REVOLUTION

BY ENRIQUE S. RIVERA

INTERNATIONAL PUBLISHERS, New York

Copyright © 2021 Enrique Rivera

All rights reserved Printed in the United States

All rights reserved. No part of this book may be reproduced or transmitted in any form or by any means, electronic or mechanical, including photo- copying, recording or any information storage retrieval system, without permission in writing from the publisher, except brief passages for review purposes.

Library of Congress Cataloging-in-Publication Data

Names: Rivera, Enrique, author.
Title: The untold history of capitalism : primitive accumulation and the anti-slavery revolution / by Enrique S. Rivera.
Description: New York : International Publishers, [2021] | Includes bibliographical references. | Summary: "This book provides a micro-history of primitive accumulation"— Provided by publisher.
Identifiers: LCCN 2021039612 (print) | LCCN 2021039613 (ebook) | ISBN 9780717808663 (paperback) | ISBN 9780717808830 (epub)
Subjects: LCSH: Capitalism. | Saving and investment. | Antislavery movements.
Classification: LCC HB501 .R566 2021 (print) | LCC HB501 (ebook) | DDC 330.12/2—dc23/eng/20211025
LC record available at https://lccn.loc.gov/2021039612
LC ebook record available at https://lccn.loc.gov/2021039613

ISBN 10: 0-7178-0866-1   ISBN-13 978-07178-0866-3
Typeset by Amnet Systems, Chennai, India

Table of Contents

Introduction 1

Chapter 1   "Precious Objects" 25

Chapter 2   Joint-Stock Company Capital 61

Chapter 3   The People 117

Chapter 4   Indigenous Labor-Power 153

Conclusion: The Conquest Continues 177

Appendix 185

Bibliography 187

Introduction

> "It is perhaps not altogether surprising that the term Capitalism, which in recent years has enjoyed so wide a currency alike in popular talk and in historical writing, should have been used so variously, and that there should have been no common measure of agreement in its use."
> —Maurice Dobb, *Studies in the Development of Capitalism* (1947)

What was true 74 years ago for the venerable economist Maurice Dobb is also true today. Despite a resurgence of talk about capitalism in Hollywood films, in the press, online, and in academia, the term remains ambiguous and its definition elusive. This book approaches this dilemma in both direct and circuitous ways. It provides a historical account of capitalism, or more appropriately, of primitive accumulation—the system that preceded capitalism and which made it possible. More indirectly, this book utilizes an anti-colonial rebellion from Venezuela in 1795—led by enslaved and legally free people of African and Indigenous descent—to tell this history of capitalism.

This is a micro-history. It takes a small-scale event to explain much larger historical phenomena. The thinking here is that if you can hone in on a local story you can provide details that more traditional histories are forced to leave out. Oftentimes, micro-history inadvertently stumbles upon findings that reshape the way we understand the past and, therefore, our present.

This book attempts to do just that. It uncovers the hidden, untold history of capitalism by detailing the minutiae from an important but understudied revolutionary movement. This insurgence erupted during that period of political upheaval known as Age of Revolution.[1] This is the epoch made famous by the Declaration of Independence (1776) and the storming of the Bastille (1789).

And then there were the 1790s—one of the most turbulent times in the history of the Americas.[2] An anti-slavery revolution engulfed the hemisphere, as conspiracy after conspiracy was uncovered and plantation after plantation went up in flames. The first match was lit on August 21, 1791, when enslaved people in the French colony of Saint-Domingue rose up in what would be known as the Haitian Revolution—the only successful slave revolt in human history.

But Haiti was not alone. Enslaved and legally free Black people in places like Brazil, Cuba, Jamaica, Louisiana and Puerto Rico also picked up arms to overthrow slavery. Most movements failed and were brutally repressed, yet there is no doubt that they hastened the fall of this abominable institution.[3]

One of the most spectacular abolitionist efforts took place in Santa Ana de Coro, in the Spanish colony of the Captaincy General of Venezuela. On the night of May 10, 1795, hundreds of enslaved and legally free people of African and native American descent revolted to topple colonial rule, eliminate slavery and taxes, and establish an independent republic. After three days of fighting—culminating in a gory conflict between as many as 450 rebels and half as many loyalists—the revolutionaries were ultimately defeated. Dozens were killed in the battlefield, and many more were callously executed in the days that followed.

---

1 The term "Age of Revolution" was coined by the late great Eric Hobsbawm: Eric J. Hobsbawm, *Age of Revolution, Europe, 1789-1848* (N.Y: Praeger Publishers, 1962).

2 This sentence was likely influenced by the following: David Barry Gaspar and David Patrick Geggus, eds., *A Turbulent Time: The French Revolution in the Greater Caribbean* (Bloomington: Indiana University Press, 1997).

3 For a recent take on this perspective, see: Tom Zoellner, *Island on Fire: The Revolt That Ended Slavery in the British Empire* (Cambridge, Mass.: Harvard University Press, 2020).

A statue of José Leonardo Chirino outside of the José Leonardo Chirino International Airport in Coro, Venezuela
Creative Commons

Nevertheless, the rebels forever altered Venezuelan history. Coro was the last bastion of royalism during the country's bloody war of independence (1810-1823), something that can be traced back to the 1795 counterrevolution.[4] The insurrectionists also inspired anti-imperialist movements in Venezuela—from 1797's Gual y España conspiracy through today's Bolivarian Revolution.[5] This book chronicles the Coro rebellion, and in the process reveals new understandings of the history of capitalism, as well as the radical notions of liberty and

---

4 John Lynch, *Simón Bolívar: A Life* (New Haven and London: Yale University Press, 2006).
5 Juan R. Lugo and Fulvia M. Polanco, *Reflexiones sobre el zambo José Leonardo y tradiciones de la sierra* (Coro, Edo. Falcón, Venezuela: Editorial Buchivacoa, 1998); Krisna Ruette-Orihuela and Cristina Soriano, "Remembering the Slave Rebellion of Coro: Historical Memory and Politics in Venezuela," *Ethnohistory* 63:2 (2016): 327-350.

equality that ended slavery, eroded monarchism, and changed the course of world history.

The 1795 Insurrection

The insurgency that shook Venezuela to its core was planned well in advance, although there are contradictory details about how it was organized and who was involved. It is clear, however, that the rebellion's leader was José Leonardo Chirino. Chirino was a legally free person classified as *zambo (or sambo)*—someone of mixed Indigenous and African descent. He was a laborer and a merchant's assistant who had traveled the circum-Caribbean quite a bit. Although Chirino was legally free, his family was not. His wife, María de los Dolores Chirino, and their three children were all enslaved.

But some were convinced that slavery's days were numbered. In fact, years before the uprising, a rumor began circulating, saying that the institution had already been abolished. According to white authorities, a legally free Black man known as Cocofío had been roaming the mountainside or *sierra*—where the region's sugar plantations were concentrated—claiming that the Spanish Crown ended slavery. He added that Coro's corrupt and nefarious officials were ignoring the edict.[6] But slavery had not been eliminated. The speculation was baseless. Cocofío died two or three years before the insurrection. Not much else is known about this mysterious figure, and he may not have even existed.

Nevertheless, the rumors continued spreading after Cocofío's death. Authorities claimed that the legally free, African-born Josef Caridad González revived the speculation. Like many Black people in Coro, González was a native of the Loango Coast. He was also the leader of Coro's large, legally free Loango community. González's

---

6 "Expediente," ff. 84. Emancipation rumors were common in anti-slavery rebellions and conspiracies during the 1790s. See: David Patrick Geggus, "Slave Resistance in the Spanish Caribbean in the Mid-1790s," in Gaspar and Geggus (1997).

Poster for Afro-Venezuelan day, celebrated annually on May 10 in commemoration of the 1795 uprising in Coro.
Courtesy of the Ministerio del Poder Popular para la Comunicación y la Información, Gobierno Bolivariano de Venezuela.

version of Cocofío's canard added that the Crown had also abolished the *alcabala*.[7] The alcabala was a tax imposed on the sale, purchase, and transport of goods. Coro's poor majority despised it, yet its exaction skyrocketed in the years leading to the rebellion.

While under duress and offering contradictory details, Chirino testified that the revolutionary cabal began conspiring the month before, at the home of a friend named Juan Bernardo Chiquito. Chirino and Chiquito later attested that they, González, and an enslaved man named Joaquín, were the only ones who knew about the rebellion in advance.[8] But at another point, Chirino also stated that González was innocent.[9] Unfortunately, only small

---

7 "Expediente," ff. 90-1.
8 "Sublevación," ff. 3-9.
9 Ibid., ff. 144-51.

fragments of Chirino's testimony exist. The document was lost many years ago and bits of it can only be gleaned from the sworn statements given by declarants who reference it.

Although facts concerning the insurrection's planning are scattered and murky, details on the rebellion itself are well documented.[10] On the night of Sunday, May 10, 1795, Chirino and four others launched the uprising on a sugar plantation called Socorro. The insurgents killed a houseguest of the property's owner, a white man named Don Josef de Martínez. After killing Martínez, the rebels stole his clothes and other valuables, and distributed them amongst themselves. They then turned their attention to the Socorro owner's son, Don Yldefonso de Tellería. The rebels attacked him and left him for dead, but the younger Tellería survived the assault.

More rebels then joined the initial band of five and began attacking neighboring plantations. Each blitz followed a similar pattern: the masters' living quarters were ransacked and slave owners were pummeled, valuable items such as textiles and fancy clothes were stolen and distributed amongst the insurgents, and sugar fields were set ablaze. From Socorro, the insurrectionists first moved to the Barón plantation owned by Doña Nicolasa Acosta—the place where Joaquín, one of the initial conspirators, lived and worked. While at Barón, they killed Don Josef María Manzanos—Acosta's lover. They then tried to take Acosta's life. They left her for dead but she survived her wounds.

The insurgents then burned Acosta's house down after robbing it, and did the same to the homes of Don Miguel de Urbina and Don Josef de Arcaya. Arcaya managed to escape and Urbina's son Manuel, who was left in charge of his father's plantation, absconded to the city of Coro. Soon after, the younger Urbina would be the first person to tell Coro's officials that an uprising was underway.

The next morning, May 11, a rebel guard intercepted one of Coro's leading men as he made his way to the

---

10 The following narrative is largely based on Mariano Ramírez Valderraín's testimony: "Expediente," ff. 1-15.

sierra. Don Joséf de Tellería owned the Socorro plantation, was Chirino's employer, and the legal owner of Chirino's family. The insurrectionists killed Tellería and his brother-in-law. They also kidnapped his wife, Doña María Josepha Rocillo, and their three children. The insurgents escorted their prisoners to a plantation known as Macanillas, which served as rebel headquarters.

Recounting that day months later, Rocillo provided one of the most intimate accounts of the insurgency. Rocillo claimed that she reprimanded Chirino, asking "how could they be so ungrateful, and traitors that Tellería being the father of all of them, they went out and killed him the same people of his house, who he loved so much and helped!"[11] Chirino replied that Tellería had told him "that he would never be governed by a sambo."[12] Rocillo responded that if Chirino's "intent was to dominate the person who said those words how could he find him after his death?"[13]

Chirino's next statement encapsulated the rebels' motivations. The leader said, "Tellería did not impede the tax collector of Coro from charging the alcabala with such excess and rigor."[14] Rocillo responded that her husband tried to address the issue through legal means. Chirino then furiously replied, "it is none of that, that the whites were in cahoots with the tax collector so that they did not have to pay, and so that all the weight of the contributions fell onto the arms of the poor, and that now either it would be repaired, or Coro would be ruined."[15]

---

[11] "Expediente," ff. 261-62: "como havian sido tan ingratos, y traidores que siendo Tellería padre de todos ellos havian salido a mattarlo los mismos de su casa, a quienes tanto amava y socorria!"

[12] Ibid., "que ningun sambo lo havia de gobernar."

[13] Ibid., "si su intentto era dominar a quien le dijo esas palabras como podia conseguirlo despues de su muertte."

[14] Ibid., "Tellería no havia impedido que el contador de Coro cobrase con tanto exceso, y rrigor las alcavalas."

[15] "Expediente," ff. 261-2: "que no era nada de eso, que los blancos estaban compuestos con el contador para no pagar ellos, y que cargase todo el peso de las contribuciones sobre los brasos de los pobres, y [folio 262] que ahora o se componia, o se arruinava Coro."

As Chirino and Rosillo exchanged words, Manuel de Urbina arrived in Coro to warn, "the blacks were coming to attack the city, sack it and kill all of the whites."[16] With this news, *Justicia Mayor* Mariano Ramírez Valderraín, Coro's sheriff, sent a message to the closest Indigenous towns—those of the Caquetío of Carrizal and Guaybacoa. He asked the loyalists to hurry. Coro was in dire straits and they needed to protect the city.

The sheriff then assembled all the people he could, along with their arms. He also ordered a force of 16 men to gather at the alcabala post of Caujarao. Caujarao was strategically located halfway between the city and the sierra so that marketers could be taxed for transporting goods between the two areas.

That same night, the conspiracy unraveled just as it was coming into fruition. González and 21 other Loangos knocked on Ramírez Valderraín's door. The men claimed that they wanted to help defend the city. They had just a few guns between them, so they asked that the sheriff hand them more. This made Ramírez Valderraín suspicious, so he locked the men up.

The sheriff's intuitions seemed to be confirmed later that night when two rebel spies were captured at Caujarao. According to officials, the men were sent from the sierra to inform González that the revolution was underway, and that they would soon advance onto the city. When word of the capture reached Ramírez Valderraín, he doubled his force at the alcabala post. But when the second detachment arrived, at around 1 a.m. on May 12, they stumbled upon a bloody scene.

The rebels had ambushed Caujarao and defeated the sheriff's first contingent. They killed two men and injured two others, one of whom would later die from his wounds. The insurgents then freed their two spies and took aim at the tax officer, *aduanista* Luis Bárcenas. The rebels broke down his doors and shattered the windows of his

---

16 Ibid., ff. 228-9: "los negros traian ánimo de asaltar a la ciudad, saquearla y matar a todos los blancos."

The sierra begins climbing at Caujarao, and extends through the Loango settlement of La Chapa, through rebel headquarters at the Macanillas plantation, and past the Indigenous town of San Luis.

home. They also taunted Bárcenas to come out "to charge the alcabala—to receive through seizure the rosaries and other personal property that he was used to taking."[17]

When Ramírez Valderraín received news of the ambush, he rallied all the white and *pardo* (Brown) men he could, along with some Caquetío from Carrizal, Guaybacoa and Santa Ana. The sheriff also grabbed two cannons, which would prove decisive. These troops held their ground until six in the morning.

At that time, over 400 men appeared on the horizon. The rebels signaled a desire to talk by waving two flags— one white and one black. They then expressed their

---

17 "Expediente," ff. 228: "a cobrar las alcabalas, a recivir en prenda los rosarios y demas muebles que acostumbrava quitar."

demands: "freedom for the slaves, exemption from the alcabala and all the other taxes on the free, and that no harm would come if we handed them the city."[18] The sheriff responded by firing a cannon filled with shrapnel. Coro's army soundly defeated the rebels that day. Although they had just 213 men, they were armed with cannons, guns, and bows and arrows. The insurgents had only machetes, lances and a few firearms. The sheriff later boasted that he killed two men with his own hands, adding, "we created a formidable carnage going after them, as many as two leagues in distance."[19] He continued, "the ones that appeared on the plains were twenty-five: the amount of blood that flowed informed of the many injured, and the fields are now sowed with bodies."[20]

During this battle, Coro's forces captured 24 rebels who were tormented before they were executed. Ramírez Valderraín claimed that all of them implicated Chirino and González as the insurrection's masterminds. They said that the plan was for Chirino's contingent to take control of the sierra as González and the Loangos took the city.

These confessions led to a wave of anti-Black violence, beginning with the murder of González and two unnamed Loangos. Having apprehended the Loangos at his home the previous day, the sheriff ordered that the prisoners be moved to the city's jail. Coro's officials later claimed that González and two other men tried to escape during this transfer, and that the guards responded by stabbing them to death.

The next morning, Wednesday, May 13, Ramírez Valderraín and his troops began making rounds to apprehend anyone considered suspicious. The following day, he sent

---

18 Ibid., ff. 22: "se les concediesela livertad a los esclavos y la exepcion de derechos de alcavala y demas impuestos a los libres, y que nada se ofreceria entregandoles asi la ciudad."

19 Ibid.: "se hizo una carniceria formidable yendo en alcanze de ellos, hasta mas de dos leguas de distancia."

20 Ibid.: "los que aparecieron en el llano fueron veinte y cinco: las señales de sangre de los que corrian, avisaban ser muchos los heridos, y asi estan los campos sembrados de cuerpos."

two expeditions, comprising 200 men each, into the sierra to announce a general amnesty. But secretly the mission also aimed to capture rebel leaders. While on these campaigns, officials murdered three suspects and captured nine more. Ramírez Valderraín had them hanged the next day, May 15. On May 18, he had 35 suspected leaders executed by gunshot. Five days later, he killed 21 more people.

Chirino fled at some point during or after the rebellion. He was discovered three months later in Baragua, 80 miles south of Coro. A man named Juan Manuel Agüero captured Chirino, who was armed with arrows and a sword.[21] For his trouble, Agüero was awarded the 100-peso bounty that was put on Chirino's head. The revolutionary leader spent the next year in jail, where he was repeatedly questioned under torturous conditions.

On December 16, 1796, Chirino was publicly executed in a grisly spectacle at Caracas's Plaza Mayor. He was hanged and his body was mutilated: his head and hands were cut off and transported to Coro. They were then displayed at various locations in the sierra.[22] As was the case in most anti-slavery insurrections, Black people in Coro felt the brunt of the suffering. The rebels killed nine people—seven white and two native American. But Ramírez Valderraín's bloodbath claimed the lives of at least 125 people of African and Afro-Indigenous descent.

The Political Economy of Coro

Eighteenth-century Coro was an extraordinary yet unremarkable place. Exceptional for its unusual topography, you can still bury yourself in dunes so extensive that you would think you're in the Sahara. Yet walk half a mile and you'll be knee-deep in the Caribbean Sea. But Coro was also conventional. Like most areas of Spain's extensive Empire, it was peripheral, sparsely populated, and economically depressed.

---

21 Ibid., ff. 10-11.
22 Ibid., ff. 1-4.

Coro's dunes.
Photo taken by author.

Throughout its post-conquest history, Coro has been jealous of its big brother Caracas, which has seemingly bullied it into forking over its most distinguished honors. Coro was Venezuela's first European settlement. Juan de Ampíes established the city in 1527 after negotiations with the Caquetío, the Arawak-speaking group that was the dominant Indigenous polity of the time. It was also the capital of Venezuela for 50 years until Caracas took its title in 1578.[23] Today, Coro is a shell of its former self. Its population of 200,000 seems paltry when compared to Venezuela's mega-metropolises and their millions of residents.

Coro's role in the world system was to produce agricultural commodities for foreign markets and to consume goods brought by Europeans.[24] The region's inhabitants

---

23 Otilia Margarita Rosas González, "La población indígena en la Provincia de Venezuela" (Ph.D. diss.: Universidad de Salamanca, 2015), 93-6.

24 The term "World System" was coined by Immanuel Wallerstein. See: Immanuel Wallerstein, *Capitalist Agriculture and the Origins of the European World-Economy in the Sixteenth Century* (New York: Academic Press, 1974).

purchased things like textiles, wigs, wines, and silverware from the continent. They also imported thousands of enslaved African people. Coro's African and Indigenous peasants and plantation workers supplied agrarian goods for domestic use and for export. Livestock, foodstuffs, and sugar were utilized in Coro, but they were also shipped to other parts of Venezuela, and to other colonies in the Caribbean.[25] Sugar, cacao, hides, and Brazil wood eventually made their way to Europe, where they served as the basis for a number of proto-industrial pursuits.[26]

Many of the products exported made their first stop in Curaçao, a tiny island that lay 60 miles off the coast of Coro. As a Dutch colony, the islet had a "free trade" policy that was radical for the time. It allowed anyone of any color or gender, representing any country or professing any religion, to trade at the port of Willemstad. This made Curaçao an attractive place for merchants big and small, and it allowed the island to dominate trade with its neighbors, including Coro.[27]

Coro's dependent economy mostly revolved around livestock.[28] The meat from bovine creatures was consumed locally and in other parts of the Captaincy General, while skins were traded in Curaçao before they were shipped to Europe. Most horses and donkeys were used domestically, but mules were exported to places like Saint-Domingue, where they powered the French colony's infamous sugar mills.[29] Farm animals were raised in two ways. One was on the haciendas owned by white élites and worked by both enslaved and legally free Black and

---

25 See chapter four for more details. Also see: Wim Klooster, "Curaçao as a Transit Center to the Spanish Main and the French West Indies," in *Dutch Atlantic Connections, 1680-1800: Linking Empires, Bridging Borders*, ed. Gert J. Oostindie and Jessica V. Roitman (Leiden and Boston: Brill, 2014), 25-51.

26 Wim Klooster, *Illicit Riches: Dutch Trade in the Caribbean, 1648-1795* (Leiden: KITLV Press, 1998), 96.

27 For a fine study on Curaçao during this period, see: Linda Rupert, *Creolization and Contraband: Curaçao in the Early Modern Atlantic World* (Athens, Ga.: University of Georgia Press, 2012).

28 See Chapter 2 for more details.

29 Klooster, "Curaçao as a Transit Center."

Indigenous individuals. Farm animals were also reared independently by Black and native American peasants.

Sugar was Coro's second major industry.[30] It was produced mainly in the sierra, where the rebellion began. White slave masters owned the region's 48 sugar plantations and employed enslaved Black people as well as legally free Black and native American workers.[31] "Free" laborers lived on plantation grounds and were paid a wage. A portion of the sweetener was consumed domestically, while another was shipped to Curaçao. Some sugar was used on the nearby island, and another portion re-exported to Amsterdam. Blocks of raw cane, known as *panelas* or *papelones*, also served as a form of currency, and legally free workers were often paid in this product.[32]

Coro exported other goods to Europe as well. Cacao was the most important cash crop for Venezuela as a whole, but it was of minor significance in Coro at the time of the insurrection.[33] Brazil wood was another important commodity. It was collected in Coro's mountains and sold to foreign merchants, most of them from Curaçao.[34]

Most legally free plantation and hacienda workers dedicated the bulk of their days not to working on plantations, but to tending their own land. Throughout the 18th century, peasants planted and harvested crops like rice, corn, cassava, and plantains. They also reared bulls, chicken, cows, donkeys, goats and mules. Products such as these were consumed at home or sold at local markets.

Part of the reason why Black and Indigenous peasants were able to operate with some independence was that

---

30 See Chapters 2 and 4 for more details.

31 "Expediente sobre la insurrección de los negros, zambos y mulatos proyectada en el año 1795 a las inmediaciones de la ciudad de Coro, Provincia de Caracas," 1795, Caracas, 426, Archivo General de Indias, Seville (AGI), ff. 1-2.

32 For an example, see: "Tocuyo: El Protector General de Indios Don Antonio Briceño, sobre el pago de tributos," 1759, Indígenas Tomo XIII, Archivo General de la Nación, Caracas (AGN).

33 "Expediente," ff. 1-2. Only seven out of Venezuela's total 95 cacao plantations were in Coro at the time of the insurrection.

34 See Chapter 2 for more details.

The Circum-Caribbean.

Coro's jurisdiction was massive and its population was sparse. This prevented landowners and colonial administrators from dominating the work routines of legally free people. This tendency was not unusual for 18th-century Venezuela, but Coro's case was still exceptional. It was one of 23 major cities and towns that made up the Captaincy General, but it held what was, by far, the largest territorial jurisdiction. The region's 26,549 inhabitants occupied 32,000 square miles. This gave it the third-largest population in Venezuela, after Caracas and La Victoria, but a land-to-person ratio of over one mile per individual.[35]

As was the case throughout Iberian America, Coro's population was segmented into racial and class categories meant to mark someone's status. Needless to say,

---

35 "Población de la Provincia de Venezuela, 1785-1787," 1787, Caracas 397, AGI. The Province of Venezuela (also known as the Province of Caracas) was one of six provinces that were united after the establishment of Venezuela as a Captaincy General. The other five provinces were those of Barinas, Guayana, Maracaibo, Nueva Andalucía (also known as Cumaná), and Mérida.

the vast majority of the region's inhabitants descended from Natives and West and West Central Africans. Most people were racially categorized as "free people of color" or pardos, and they numbered nearly 12,000 or approximately 44% of the population.[36] The second largest group were "free Indians," Caquetíos who were exempt from tribute payments because of their loyalty to the Spanish Crown. The Caquetío numbered over 7,000, or 26% of residents. They mostly lived in the towns scattered along the Caribbean coast and in the Peninsula of Paraguaná.[37]

The third-biggest class were whites, which numbered 3,700 or nearly 14% of the population.[38] Most were native-born and descended from Spaniards. It is likely that some of those classified as "white" were also of partial native American and/or African descent. Many of the white militia members of the neighboring Province of Maracaibo, for example, were described as *"trigueño"* or "wheat-colored" in 1787.[39] The fourth-largest grouping were enslaved people of African descent who numbered over 3,200, equaling about 12% of the population. Most enslaved people toiled on plantations, although a relative few worked as domestic servants.

Finally, there were the Ajaguas and Ayamanes, the unfree Indigenous people who numbered 768, or 3% of residents.[40] These groups were not considered free

---

36 "Sublevación de los negros de Coro, pieza 1," 1795, Criminales Letra C, AGN. *Pardo* literally translates to Brown. It is generally understood that *pardos* in colonial Venezuela were people of mixed African and European descent. It is important to note, however, that the term *negro*, or black, was used only when referring to enslaved people. In addition, *mestizo* was a term rarely used in Coro. This may be because many mestizos were categorized as white. Given the large number of native American people in Coro, however, it is probable that many *pardos* were also of mixed indigenous and African descent. The often-used category *zambo* is not used in the population censuses, and therefore *zambos* fell under the category of *pardos*.
37 Ibid.
38 "Sublevación de los negros, pieza 1," ff. 1.
39 "Revista de Inspección de la Tropa Veterana y de Milicias de Maracaibo," 1787, SGU 7198, 18, Archivo General de Simancas, Spain.
40 "Sublevación de los negros, pieza 1," ff. 1.

because they were responsible for making costly tribute payments to the Crown. Most of these communities were concentrated in Coro's sierra, and west of it. The greatest assemblages of Ajaguas were in San Luis, Pecaya, and Pedregal. Like the Caquetío, the Ajaguas were Arawak speakers, while the Ayamanes spoke Jirajara. Coro's Indigenous peoples settled in the region 10,000-12,000 years ago.[41]

Most of Coro's rebels were of African descent. As was the case throughout the Americas, Black people lived in Coro because of their enslavement or that of their ancestors. They had origins throughout the African continent, although the vast majority came from the West and West Central regions. The Gold Coast of Guinea (contemporary Ghana) and the Loango Coast of West Central Africa (a coastline that stretches through parts of contemporary Angola, Gabon, and the Republic of the Congo) were the two leading places of origin for Coro's Black people.[42]

The political economy of Coro was geared toward serving the interests of European and white creole élites. The region imported European manufactures, as well as enslaved African people, and produced agricultural commodities that were shipped to neighboring colonies and to Europe. Many of the goods exported were harvested on Coro's haciendas and plantations. But despite the fact that thousands of people of African and Indigenous descent were coerced into laboring on these estates, most

---

[41] Jossy M. Mansur, *E indiannan Caquetío* (Aruba: Imprenta Nacional Arubano, 1981), 29; Willem F.H. Adelaar, *The Languages of the Andes* (Cambridge: Cambridge University Press, 2004), 129.

[42] The SSC held the *asiento* for the Spanish Crown between 1715-39, and provided many of the enslaved people of Coro. Just over 23% of people enslaved by the SSC had origins on the Gold Coast, while 32.8% had origins in the Loango Coast. It is likely, however, that the Dutch illegally provided most enslaved people to 18th-century Coro. After the English *asiento*, 33% percent of enslaved people purchased by the Dutch were from the Gold Coast, while 37% were from the Loango Coast, making 70% of enslaved people procured by the Dutch having origins in one of the two regions. See: Alex Borucki, "Trans-imperial History in the Making of the Slave Trade to Venezuela, 1526-1811." *Itinerario* 36:2 (2012): 29-54.

of Coro's population was able to plant, harvest, and trade with only limited state interference. This would change in the 1790s, and Coro would be burned to the ground.

Interventions

Most people like to think in determinisms. We often search for *the* cause of any given phenomenon, as if there is *one* thing—a magic bullet—that can explain why something is happening. But historically, as well as today, we know that numerous factors work together to produce any given action or event.

Let's take the example of former U.S. President Donald Trump and some comments he made about Venezuela, the country whose history we are discussing here. In an interview with *Axios*, Trump told the publication that he would be willing to talk to Venezuelan President Nicolás Maduro.[43] This was an about-face on the U.S. policy of attacking Venezuela from all angles and refusing to dialogue with a government it has targeted for régime change. As soon as Trump's statement made the rounds, his 2020 opponent Joe Biden and U.S. media outlets blasted him for his willingness to negotiate. Then something curious happened: Trump backtracked. He quickly announced that he would only talk to Maduro if he resigned.

Why did Trump change his mind? Many political analysts suggested it had everything to do with Florida. With the 2020 presidential elections around the corner, Trump felt he needed to win the swing state to win the national election. In order to do that, so the story went, he needed to keep Miami's hard-right Cuban and Venezuelan expatriate communities happy. And they would not be happy if he seemed "soft" on Venezuela.

Miami's hardliners certainly had something to do with it, but other conditions also played a part. First

---

[43] "Exclusive: Trump cold on Guaidó, would consider meeting Maduro," in *Axios*, published June 21, 2020. https://www.axios.com/trump-venezuela-guaido-maduro-ea665367-b088-4900-8d73-c8fb50d96845.html

the obvious, and perhaps the most important: Venezuela holds the largest proven oil reserves on the planet and has an abundance of other natural resources. The Bolivarian Revolution established an alternative political and economic system that saw a great deal of success for a number of years. Venezuela has also denounced U.S. imperial actions across the globe, forged alliances with other "rogue" states and entities, and threatened to squeeze the United States out of Venezuela's markets. Given this, the Pentagon, as well as their partners in the oil, weapons, and tech industries, would not have been very happy with Trump's remarks.

But there were other concerns as well. How effectively might the Democratic Party be able to use Trump's statement to smear him and his campaign? This points to the question of Trump's base of support and its tendency to harbor Cold War-era nationalist and anti-communist sentiment. And let's not forget their racism toward Brown people in general, which certainly influences the way they see Venezuela and its government.

So as can be seen, even critical pundits oversimplified the situation and failed to explain why Trump retracted his statement. It wasn't *just* about Florida. Besides, most Cuban-American voters no longer hold such a hard line. The greater part favors normalizing relations with Cuba and supports ending the U.S. blockade against the island.[44]

All social phenomena are the product of multiple objective and subjective conditions that converge to make things happen. This work provides more evidence for this truism.[45] Various factors combined to create the Coro that went up in flames in 1795. This book explores some of them while providing two original, interconnected assertions.

---

44 "2018 FIU Cuba Poll: How Cuban Americans in Miami View U.S. Policies Towards Cuba," *Steven J. Green School of International and Public Affairs.* https://cri.fiu.edu/research/cuba-poll/2018-fiu-cuba-poll.pdf, Accessed September 4, 2020.

45 Louis Althusser's work has been key to this conceptualization. See: Louis Althusser, *For Marx* (London and New York: Verso, 2005).

The first argument has to do with capitalism. As we saw in the opening epigraph, the term induces confusion across the political spectrum. So, what is capitalism? Does it have to do with markets? With trade? Private vs. public? Money? Investments? No, not really. Money, markets, and investments have existed all over the world and for millennia. If these characteristics are considered the basis of capitalism, then medieval Europe, as well as their contemporaries in Mesoamerica, the Andes, Ghana, and Benin should also be considered capitalist. Not to mention ancient Greece, Rome, and Egypt. If everything is capitalism then nothing is capitalism.

But capitalism is a real political and economic system that was formed at a specific time and in a particular place. Capitalism has a history. But this begs the question, what is that history? When did it begin?

Let's first review what "it" is. Capitalism is an economic system based on a distinct mode of production. Its method presupposes that laborers are divorced from the means of subsistence and the means of production. In other words, capitalism is based on the fact that workers cannot feed or clothe themselves without toiling for a wage. They then use this wage to purchase their necessities. Under capitalism, laborers also lack ownership over the land, tools and/or machines with which they work. This prevents them from laboring on their own accord. Now that the workers cannot labor for themselves, nor feed, clothe or house themselves, they are entirely dependent on a capitalist class in order to survive. The only thing they can do to sustain themselves is sell their labor, i.e., work for a wage. With these wages, they are able to purchase their subsistence. This is capitalism.[46] And it's the most dynamic political and economic system ever known. It may also be the most destructive.

---

46 See, in particular, Chapter 6 in Marx's *Capital*, vol. 1, "The Sale and Purchase of Labour-Power" in Karl Marx, *Capital, Volume 1* (New York: Penguin Books, 1990), 270-80.

So when did capitalism come about? Well, this is one of this book's primary interventions. Karl Marx dated the dawn of capitalism to the 16th century.[47] Historians, whether Marxist or not, have been influenced by this periodization. But my research throws this timetable into question. This is where the unintended consequences of micro-history provide another gem. While investigating the ground-level operations of the European industries that shaped Coro and the 1795 insurrection, I discovered that they were not capitalist. More specifically, while providing details on the textile industries in contemporary England, Belgium, and France, I found that these were based on the work of peasants who controlled their means of production and subsistence. This is a far cry from capitalist industry. In addition, my research into the joint-stock companies that shaped Coro showed all the signs of a feudal economy rather than a capitalist one.

Therefore, I argue that it was primitive accumulation that gave rise to Coro's plantation economy and the revolutionary movement that aimed to destroy it.[48] Marx's

---

47 Marx, 876.

48 It's important to note that these conclusions are preliminary. More research into the development of capitalism in Great Britain is needed, but there are reasons to doubt the conventional wisdom. Joseph Inikori, for example, has shown that that it was not until 1801-03 that wage-laborers in agriculture began to exceed the number of farmers in England by a count of 340,000 families to 320,000 families [Joseph Inikori, *Africans and the Industrial Revolution in England: A Study in International Trade and Economic Development* (New York: Cambridge University Press, 2002, 45)]. Robert Brenner's foundational work on the subject defines early modern agriculture in Great Britain as capitalist, yet he emphasizes that agricultural workers still had access to the means of production. Brenner departs from Marx's conception of capitalism by deemphasizing the importance of means of production, arguing for the more significant role played by market dependence in the historical development of capitalism. With all due respect to Prof. Brenner, I am loyal to Marx's conception of capitalism, and stress the significance of *dependence on a capitalist employer* to the functioning of this mode of production. Usurping the means of production prevents workers from laboring on their own accord, from dictating their pace of work, and from controlling the product they produce. Without controlling the means of production, lords and masters lack one of the two essential prerequisites needed to make workers dependent on them to survive. Therefore, I contend that market dependence alone is not enough to produce capitalism, and similar dependencies have been seen in prior epochs and in different regions of the world. Although often

notion of a prior accumulation, which made capitalism possible, was a takeoff from Adam Smith's analysis of the same. In Marx's conception, the enclosure of peasant land in early modern England, as well as the conquest of the Americas, the Atlantic slave trade, and African slavery in the Western Hemisphere, all provided the conditions that made capitalism possible.[49] This is the process that created places like Coro, and gave rise to the antislavery revolution.

This book's second major contention has to do with rebel ideology. I argue that the peasant economies of Coro and West and West Central Africa inspired the insurgents' revolutionary ideas. Historians tend to credit the egalitarian beliefs emanating out the European Atlantic—such as "all men are created equal"—as inspiring the wave of anti-slavery insurrection that gripped the

---

looking like capitalism, I would argue that the early modern period should be better understood as the period of primitive accumulation—the transition from feudalism to capitalism; the process that made capitalism possible, but does not in itself constitute capitalism.

Recent years have seen an explosion of literature on racial capitalism, a term popularized by the late Cedric Robinson and his great work *Black Marxism*. Influenced by Robinson's analysis, this literature has shed light on the fundamental role that ideas about race have had on capitalist work regimes, as well as exposed the material foundations of white privilege—what Cheryl Harris has perhaps more appropriately called "whiteness as property." Although I am convinced that there is a racial/global division of labor in the modern world, I am not convinced that this is unique to capitalism, as some writers—although not Robinson—contend. Nor am I convinced that a racial division of labor is reproduced wherever capitalist relations exist, as Robinson and others allude. I do think, however, that the term is a useful one, particularly when applied to specific circumstances. See the work of Peter Hudson and Martin Legassick and David Hemson for examples.

Recently, John Clegg has argued that slavery in the U.S. South was a capitalist enterprise. I would counter his position that plantation owners were capitalists because they were dependent on the market, by saying that feudal lords were as well. In addition, the workers were obviously not paid a wage, and this is important because they were not forced to purchase their means of subsistence. They were either given these by their legal master or forced to grow and manufacture them themselves. It is important to note that, as a consequence, enslaved workers were not dynamic consumers whose subsistence needs could rapidly increase over time, as is of the utmost importance under capitalism.

49 See Part 8 of *Capital* on "So-Called Primitive Accumulation," Marx, 873-938.

Americas during the Age of Revolution.[50] Indeed, the circulation, popularization and Europeanization of these ideas were important. But by closely studying the words and actions of Coro's rebels alongside the political and economic customs of their homelands, I found that the latter were crucial in animating the radical notions of equality that the rebels espoused.

This book provides a micro-history of primitive accumulation. It tells the story of how the yin of European imperialism, conquest, and slavery confronted the yang of communitarian societies in Africa and the Americas. This is the untold history of capitalism.

---

50 David Patrick Geggus, *Slavery, War, and Revolution: The British Occupation of Saint Domingue, 1793-1798* (Oxford: Clarendon Press, 1982); David Patrick Geggus, *Haitian Revolutionary Studies* (Bloomington: Indiana University Press, 2002); Gaspar and Geggus (1997); David Patrick Geggus and Norman Fiering, *The World of the Haitian Revolution* (Bloomington: Indiana University Press, 2009); David Scott, *Conscripts of Modernity: The Tragedy of Colonial Enlightenment* (Durham: Duke University Press, 2004); Laurent Dubois, *Avengers of the New World: The Story of the Haitian Revolution* (Cambridge, Mass.: Belknap Press of Harvard University Press, 2004); Laurent Dubois, *A Colony of Citizens: Revolution and Slave Emancipation in the French Caribbean, 1787-1804* (Chapel Hill: University of North Carolina Press, 2004); Ada Ferrer, *Freedom's Mirror: Cuba and Haiti in the Age of Revolution* (New York: Cambridge University Press, 2014); Nick Nesbitt, *Universal Emancipation: The Haitian Revolution and the Radical Enlightenment* (Charlottesville: University of Virginia Press, 2008); Susan Buck-Morss, *Hegel, Haiti and Universal History* (Pittsburgh: University of Pittsburgh Press, 2009); Doris Garraway, ed., *Tree of Liberty: Cultural Legacies of the Haitian Revolution in the Atlantic World* (Charlottesville: University of Virginia Press, 2008); David P. Geggus and Norman Fiering, eds., *The World of the Haitian Revolution* (Bloomington: Indiana University Press, 2009); David Scott, *Conscripts of Modernity: The Tragedy of Colonial Enlightenment* (Durham: Duke University Press, 2004); Matt Childs, *The 1812 Aponte Rebellion in Cuba and the Struggle Against Atlantic Slavery* (Chapel Hill: University of North Carolina Press, 2006).

Chapter 1

"Precious Objects"

Months after the insurrection, jurist Don Juan Estevan de Valderrama arrived in Coro at the behest of the Spanish Crown. He was tasked with leading an investigation into the rebellion—what happened, why it happened, and what had happened since. What he uncovered was a conspiracy that terrified an incipient nation, an uprising that rocked established hierarchies, and a society whose foundations of race and class were mediated by the uses and abuses of European cloth.[51]

Valderrama, a Castilian trained in civil and canonical law, had spent the past two decades serving in various government posts in the Province of Maracaibo. By the time Coro had gone up in flames, the irascible failed priest had reached the apex of any stately gentleman's career. He was currently serving as the Governor of Maracaibo and the Lieutenant Governor of the entire Captaincy General. Valderrama only answered to one man in Spain's burgeoning colony, and that was Don Pedro de Carbonell, the Captain General himself and the Governor of Caracas.

Valderrama arrived on the night of October 3, 1795, after Carbonell called for his assistance six weeks before. He stated that he needed Valderrama in Coro because local authorities there had "grave difficulties" telling

---

[51] "Expediente sobre la insurrección de los negros, zambos y mulatos proyectada en el año 1795 a las inmediaciones de la ciudad de Coro, Provincia de Caracas," 1795, Caracas, 426, AGI, ff. 193.

25

him what transpired during the rebellion as well as where things currently stood.[52] According to Carbonell, this poor record of communication had the dangerous potential of "confusing the innocent with the true criminals of this case."[53] Therefore, the inquiry needed to be "conducted by an outsider of that jurisdiction, of known integrity, expertise, maturity and advice."[54] The well-bred, no-nonsense Valderrama was the perfect man for the job.

Carbonell distrusted Coro's officials, particularly its venal and equally vicious sheriff Don Mariano Ramírez Valderraín. In essence, Valderrama would replace the disgraced leader. His mission was to do what the sheriff should have done months before: determine who was involved in the rebellion and who was not.

One key to identifying who was truly guilty or innocent was to uncover what happened with the European textiles and luxurious clothes that were stolen from wealthy whites during the insurrection. As was the case throughout the Atlantic, European linen held a great deal of material and symbolic value in 18th-century Coro. These cloths were imported to manufacture clothes, which served as markers of élite racial and class status. From the very start of the rebellion, clothes, clothing articles, and other valuables were stolen from plantations, and even off the corpse of one of the rebels' victims.

Scores of witnesses and accused insurgents were called to testify before Valderrama. Many were asked about the status of textiles, clothes, and other valuables that had been looted. Some deponents had been incarcerated in Coro's infamously unkempt and rotting prison since the earliest days of the uprising. Others were called in for questioning and showed up "voluntarily."

---

52 Ibid., 116: "graves dificultades."
53 Ibid.
54 Ibid.: "de confundir los inocenttes con los verdaderos reos de esta causa, sino se pone la substtanciacion de ella a cargo de persona forastera de aquella jurisdicion y de conocida provedad, ciencia, madures y consejo.

One person who arrived at court, supposedly on her own volition, was 45-year-old María de los Dolores Chirino. She was married to José Leonardo Chirino, the alleged leader of the insurrection. María de los Dolores lived a difficult life. She was born enslaved—the legal property of the landowner, merchant, and Crown bureaucrat Joséf de Tellería. Although her husband was legally free, her three children were, like her, born enslaved because slavery was inherited by way of the mother in Venezuela, as it was throughout the Americas.[55]

Evidence suggests that Chirino and her family were close to the Tellerías. José Leonardo was known as Joséf de Tellería's right-hand man. He traveled with him to nearby Curaçao on several occasions and to Saint-Domingue as well. María de los Dolores, José Leonardo, and their children all lived inside the master's quarters at Socorro. It was one of the three plantations that Tellería owned, and the one where the May rebellion began.

On October 23, 1795, María de los Dolores Chirino gave Valderrama invaluable details on what transpired the first night of the rebellion, specifics that only she could provide. She testified that on the night of May 10, she was serving dinner to Don Joséph Nicolás Martínez, a houseguest of the Tellería family. She said that a girl interrupted her work by telling her that people were fighting outside. Chirino said that she asked the youngster if her husband was involved, and that the child responded that she did not know. As Chirino kept attending to Martínez, the child interrupted two more

---

[55] Most historical analysis on the role of women's bodies in reproducing enslaved labor has focused on Anglophone America. These insights are easily applicable to the rest of the continent, however. See: Hilary McD. Beckles, *Natural Rebels: A Social History of Enslaved Black Women in Barbados* (New Brunswick, N.J.: Rutgers University Press, 1989); Angela Y. Davis, *Women Race & Class* (New York: Vintage Books, 1983); Jennifer L. Morgan, *Laboring Women: Reproduction and Gender in New World Slavery* (Philadelphia: University of Pennsylvania Press, 2004); Jennifer L. Morgan, "Partus Sequitur Ventrem: Law, Race, and Reproduction in Colonial Slavery," *Small Axe* 22.1 (2018): 1-17.

times. It was during the third interposition that Chirino decided to investigate for herself.

Chirino testified that she found her husband outside drunk. She said that she scolded him, "Is it possible that you are this way when you must leave at dawn to receive my master Don Joséf Tellería?"[56] Chirino returned to the kitchen and served Martínez his food. She told him that she did not dare "bring him the coffee because with Leonardo being in the disposition that he is in, she distrusted to go out for it."[57]

Chirino then described in detail how she witnessed Martínez's murder. She said that she was so frightened by her husband's behavior that she hid in a bedroom near the kitchen. Suddenly, Chirino saw her husband standing next to the door, accompanied by six other men, and holding an unsheathed sword. She said that she then ran out of the house to hide, when a mortally wounded Martínez approached her, telling her to escape to Tellería's other plantation, La Asunción. According to Chirino, Martínez stated that he could not escape with her because "he was already injured, that he could not."[58] Sadly, Chirino's next recorded statement would seal her tragic fate:

> the insurgents had just taken the life of Martínez, as the declarant witnessed, in the same place where he was left, and Leonardo divided up his clothes amongst themselves, but she does not know whether they also divided up the clothing articles or money that he had, because in regards to this, she does not know what was done with them.[59]

---

[56] "Expediente," ff. 303.: "es possible estés de esa manera deviendo salir de madrugada a recivir a mi amo Don Joséph Tellería."
[57] Ibid.: "a traerle el café por que estando Leonardo en la disposicion que se hallava se recelava salir por el."
[58] Ibid.: "ya estaba herido que no podia."
[59] Ibid.: "los insurgentes acabaron de quitar la vida a Martínez como lo vió la que declara en el mismo parage en donde lo dejó, y entre ellos repartió sus bestidos Leonardo, pero no save si tambien las prendas o dinero que tendria, pues de esto no esta entendida que se hizo."

Chirino went home after this initial testimony, but she was arrested two weeks later. Valderrama accused her of lying before the court and ordered her apprehension. The gentleman's suspicions arose on November 7 when Don Juan Francisco Santaliz, a white landowner in Coro's Indigenous village of Pedregal, gave his testimony. Santaliz attested that in the aftermath of the rebellion, he pressured Chirino and her children to disclose where her husband was hiding. He threatened to whip them if they did not divulge his location. Santaliz did not say whether or not he beat Chirino or her children, but he revealed that he had confiscated a host of stolen goods from her, which included textiles and clothes.[60]

Two days later, Chirino was arrested and charged as a rebel. Valderrama believed that the truth behind the extent of her involvement lay in her suppression of key details. Why had she neglected to mention that her husband had given her some of Martínez's clothes after he was killed? Why did she also say that she had no idea if José Leonardo had distributed linens or other articles of clothing, when she had some in her possession just days after the rebellion?[61]

But Chirino was not the only person whose testimony about stolen textiles landed them in hot water. Juan de Jesús de Lugo, an Indigenous man from the tribute-paying town of Pecaya, had been jailed in the aftermath of the insurrection, implicated by José Leonardo himself. The 31-year-old Lugo had been incarcerated for five months before he testified before Valderrama. Like María de los Dolores, Lugo denied being involved in the uprising. According to him, the opposite was true. Coro's rebels tried to kill *him*, Lugo claimed, because they accused him of fighting "in defense of the whites."[62]

---

60 "Expedientes, sublevación de esclavos en la sierra de Coro, 1795," 1795, Judiciales, A16-C54-D11183, Academia Nacional de Historia, Caracas, ff. 1-3.
61 Ibid., ff. 13-14.
62 Ibid., 186.: "en defensa de los blancos."

Lugo held that his run-in with the rebellion began when he left home for work the morning after it was launched. While on his way, Lugo ran into Juan del Carmen Rivero, a man racially classified as pardo. According to Lugo, Rivero told him to go home because "the blacks are revolting."[63] Lugo stated that soon after he returned, he came across a group of rebels who beat him up.

Severely battered, Lugo managed to escape by entering the home of an elderly landowner named Doña Concepción Suárez. Lugo then attested that the rebels wanted to kill Suárez and steal her belongings. He reacted by helping her grab a hammock and fill it with clothes and other goods that belonged to her. In order to prevent her valuables from being stolen, he then hid them outside of his home.[64]

Lugo testified that he then went to the Quitaragua plantation to warn its elderly owner Doña Ana Vera. Lugo said that he did this so that she could escape, as well as hide her clothes, textiles, and other wares from the rebels. But by the time he arrived, the insurgents had already "sacked the house."[65] Vera survived unscathed and, according to Lugo, she handed him a bag so that he could go to her other home in San Luis to recover her most valuable possessions.

But when Lugo got to San Luis, Cristóbal Acosta, an infamous insurrectionist whom authorities considered to be José Leonardo's "captain," was already distributing Vera's clothes to his contingent. Lugo said that when he realized that these were Vera's belongings, he stuffed them into the bag she had given him.[66] Despite the passion with which he defended himself, Valderrama was deeply suspicious of Lugo's declaration. So the judge called a number of witnesses to corroborate it. Things would not end well for the accused.

---

63 Ibid., 184: "los negros estan sublevados."
64 Ibid.
65 Ibid.: "saqueado la casa."
66 Ibid., 187.

The sworn statements given by Chirino and Lugo show that clothes and clothing articles were of great import for Coro's revolutionaries. From the moment the insurrection was launched, the rebels, led by José Leonardo, stole Martínez's clothes, textiles, and other valuables after they stabbed him to death. As María de los Dolores testified, her husband then distributed these goods to the six men with him. As would later be made clear, however, the rebel leader also gave some to his wife. Likewise, Lugo's declaration reveals how insurgents in San Luis, led by Chirino's "captain" Acosta, stole clothes while burglarizing the homes of oligarchic whites. Like Chirino, Acosta distributed these valuables to the insurrectionists who accompanied him.

Being indignant about the racial-class polarity of the world they lived in, Coro's revolutionaries saw textiles as one of the ways in which this inequity manifested itself. For the rebels, Martínez was an embodiment of their oppressor. He was a prosperous white man who held the privileges of his caste—the ability to live comfortably, be attended to by servants, bark orders, and whip whichever enslaved person he wished.

As poor people of African and Indigenous descent, Coro's insurgents were trapped in a life in which they worked for men like Martínez. When the insurrectionists killed Martínez, they felt they were murdering Coro's racial-class system. When the rebels stole his clothes, they continued in the unraveling of Coro's society. Martínez's garments, his textiles, and his luxury items were so significant that they fused to the bedrock of Coro's plantation economy, the very system which sustained these inequalities. By stealing his belongings, Coro's rebels were upending society, making what was his, theirs.

By distributing these goods amongst themselves, the most romantic dreamers among Coro's revolutionaries were further chastising the region's socioeconomic structure. The act of redistribution was the symbolic declaration of their own moral code, which was the opposite of their oppressors. For the most idealistic rebels, reallocation served to legitimate this value system, which would be the foundation for their new society.

Surviving records of the insurrection also reveal an obsession with textiles and clothes on the part of Valderrama and colonial authorities. For the white ruling class, European fabrics and luxurious garments were a means to an end—status symbols that they dedicated their lives to accumulate and to display. Likewise, opulent outfits made of European cloth were markers of whiteness, a rare and highly valued currency in Coro.[67]

When Santaliz discovered European textiles, clothes, and other valuables in the possession of María de los Dolores, he confidently confiscated them, knowing that these magnificent items could not belong to a Black slave. When Santaliz threatened to whip Chirino if she did not reveal where her husband was hiding, he was threatening to punish her for her dissent. In Santaliz's eyes, Chirino's possession of European fabrics was a crime in and of itself. It was an act of subversion that threatened to blur the line between the powerful and the powerless. When Valderrama had Chirino arrested for lying under oath, it was her temporary possession of white garments that threatened the hegemonic order just as much as her lying in court did.[68]

The centrality of European textiles points to the convoluted network of production and consumption, semiotics and political economy, which created the Atlantic world.[69] This chapter explores the material reality that interfaced

---

[67] For a theoretical discussion of whiteness as a form of property, see: Cheryl I. Harris, "Whiteness As Property," *Harvard Law Review*, 106.8 (1993): 1707-1791.

[68] For hegemony, see Gramsci's definition in Quintin Hoare and Geoffrey Nowell Smit, ed., trans., *Selections from the Prison Notebooks of Antonio Gramsci* (New York: International Publishers, 1971), 12.

[69] For a critique of the literature on the Atlantic World see: Enrique Salvador Rivera, "Whitewashing the Dutch Atlantic." *Social and Economic Studies* 64:1 (2015): 117-132.

with the language of European cloth.[70] The clothes and fabrics that Coro's rebels stole and hid, and the ones that authorities were obsessed to find, were one of the pillars of a political economy that connected European peasants to merchants, and these traders to producers and consumers in Africa and the Americas. This chapter seeks to uncover why textiles and clothes were so consequential. It starts by investigating where they were made, how they were made, and how they arrived in Coro. It illustrates that European fabrics were infused with a complex of social relations that shaped the nature of race, class, and revolution in the 18th-century Atlantic.

Textiles and Clothing in 18th-Century Coro

One Sunday morning in 1774, María Francisca de la Peña and her daughters, who were all racially and sexually categorized as *mulatas*, went to church in the city of Coro.[71] This was a noteworthy social event, as all three women wore *alfombras*, highly coveted sheets made of silk and wool, which covered their heads, draped over their shoulders, and blanketed their torsos.[72] But because they were caught wearing these items, de la Peña and her daughters were arrested and would soon face trial. According to the *Leyes de las Indias*—the Laws of the Indies—women of African descent were not allowed to

---

70 This position is inspired by many works, including the following: Louis Althusser, *For Marx* (London and New York: Verso, 2005); Stuart Hall, "The Problem of Ideology—Marxism without Guarantees." Journal of Communication Inquiry, 10:2 (1986): 28-44; Stuart Hall, "Gramsci's Relevance for the Study of Race and Ethnicity." Journal of Communication Inquiry, 10:2 (1986), 5-27; V.N. Vološinov, *Marxism and the Philosophy of Language* (Cambridge, Mass., and London: Harvard University Press, 1973).

71 Neruska Rojas, "Las criollas y sus trapos: matices de la moda femenina caraqueña durante la segunda mitad del siglo XVIII," in *Se acata pero no se cumple: historia y sociedad en la Provincia de Caracas (siglo XVIII)* (Caracas: Academia Nacional de la Historia, 2014), ed. by Neller Ramón Ochoa Hernández and Jorge Flores González, 275.

72 "Alfombra," in Real Academia Española, Diccionario de la lengua castellana, 1791.

wear expensive jewelry, blankets, or any other luxury articles, unless they were married to a Spaniard.[73]

During the trial of de la Peña and her daughters, a Crown lawyer expressed disquiet about Black people wearing European clothes. His chief concern was that it blurred hierarchies of race and class. But he also critiqued what, in his mind, was the deterioration of continental style:

> The mulatas compete with each other during the day to see who can best annul the grace of the alfombra, and because it would look very bad with a wool skirt, a garment considered primitive by the higher classes; out comes the haggler with the ugly combination of a necklace, gold bracelets, pearls, or precious stones, with the most decorated velvet overskirt, cloth slippers, etc.[74]

Coro's authorities wanted to make an example of de la Peña and her daughters. Although the outcome of their trial is unknown at this time, the scandal did result in an attempt to more strictly prohibit Black people from wearing luxurious garments. Officers soon posted a notice in Coro's central plaza, stating that the breaking of this law would result in a 25 peso fine for a first offense. A second offense would prompt another 25 peso fine, plus six months of community service, and any other penalty deemed appropriate by officials.[75]

Opulent clothes were available in Coro because of the growth of its plantation economy and the changing fortunes of European empires. The production of Venezuelan

---

73 Cited in Rojas, 250; Leyes de Indias, Tomo VII, Título Quinto. De los Mulatos, Negros, Berberiscos, é hijos de Indios, "Ley xxviii. Que las Negras, y Mulatas borras no traigan oro, seda, mantos, ni perlas."

74 Ibid., 276. "Las mulatas a competencia se abrogan en el dia la gracia de la alfombra, y como pareceria muy mal con una saya de lana un traje privativo en nuestras leyes a determinados papeles; sale la regatona con el gerolifico de punta, collar, manillas de oro, perlas, o piedras preciosas con los mas atavios de basquina de terclopelo, chapines de tela, etc."

75 Ibid.

cacao grew rapidly throughout the 18th century. As output expanded, trade increased, along with the purchasing power of propertied people, who squandered much of their wealth on ostentation.[76] This brashness was buttressed by the rising predominance of the French Empire and the Spanish Crown's transition from the Hapsburg Dynasty to that of the Bourbons at the turn of the century. At this time, the flamboyant style of the French upper class became a fad in the Spanish Atlantic, replacing the more Spartan clothing of previous generations.[77] Consumption of French and other European textiles in Venezuela grew further after the establishment of the Real Compañía Guipuzcoana (RCG)—the Royal Guipuzcoan Company—in 1730. This corporation was able to provide a steady influx of European products during the 55 years in which it operated.[78]

European travelers were dazzled by the clothing of the wealthy in Venezuela. Some years after the insurrection, Frenchman F. Depons noted, "Laces also form a part of the Spanish dress; those of Flanders obtain the preference."[79] Depons added, "there are few whites who are not dressed in ash coloured or blue casimere."[80] Another French visitor, Louis Alexandre Berthier, noted in 1783, "'first class men' were 'dressed as in Spain.'"[81] Berthier gushed over the beauty and "sumptuousness" of élite Venezuelan women whose affluence and appreciation of fashion allowed them to wear as many as three outfits in one day: one in which they went to church, a second that they wore while at home, and a third in which they went dancing.[82]

---

76 Carlos F. Duarte, *Historia del traje durante la época colonial venezolana* (Caracas: Armitano, 1984), 58.
77 Ibid., 57.
78 Ibid.
79 F. Depons, *Travels in Parts of South America, during the years 1801, 1802, 1803 & 1804*, vol. 2 (London: Richard Phillips, 1806), 332.
80 Ibid., 333.
81 Ibid., 124: "los hombres 'de primera clase' estaban 'vestidos como en España.'"
82 Ibid., 134.

By contrast, the outfits worn by people of African and Indigenous descent were more threadbare. Berthier mentioned that there were three categories of people below "pure-blooded" Spaniards in Caracas: the second class was *mestizos*, the third was Indigenous, and the fourth was Black. Mestizos, Berthier noted, dressed similarly to Europeans, although their garments were made of inexpensive textiles. Indigenous people tried to imitate mestizos the best they could, although they were not allowed to wear black shawls to church, and could only wear white veils. The fourth class, people of African descent, only wore a shirt, a skirt, and a handkerchief on top of their heads. The wealthier Black people would wear large gold earrings.[83] Enslaved people dressed in few items, and they were usually made of cotton or animal skins.[84]

This is not to say, however, that people of African and native American descent did not ignore law and custom to dress in the style of gaudy white oligarchs. On the contrary, European dress could be used as a means of social mobility for nonwhite people. In 18th-century Mexico, Peru, and Saint-Domingue, for example, European visitors were appalled to see people of African and Indigenous descent wearing the same clothes worn by wealthy whites.[85] It is unlikely that Venezuelan authorities could completely control the use of luxurious clothing by Black and Indigenous people. This was particularly true for those nonwhites who made up the vast majority of society's middle strata. As seen in the episode with de la Peña and her daughters, however, colonial officials did enforce this law when they found it in their interest to do so.

---

83 Ibid., 135-6.
84 Ibid., 201.
85 Rebecca Earle, "Luxury, Clothing and Race in Colonial Spanish America," in *Luxury in the Eighteenth Century: Debates, Desires and Delectable Goods*, ed. Maxine Berg and Elizabeth Eger (New York: Palgrave, 2003); Tamara J. Walker, *Exquisite Slaves: Race, Clothing, and Status in Colonial Lima* (New York: Cambridge University Press, 2017); Joan Dayan, *Haiti, History, and the Gods* (Berkeley: University of California Press, 1995), 170-82.

Although textiles were imported from Europe, clothes—such as the alfombras worn by de la Peña and her family—were manufactured locally. They were made in boutiques, which were owned by master tailors, usually men of African descent who employed enslaved apprentices. In the largest shops, there would be a master couturier, five other clothiers and two enslaved trainees.[86] To become a tailor, one had to register with the local guild, pay a registration fee, and pass examinations.[87] Elites would meet with their outfitters after they purchased their textiles at the market or in a local store. They would then tell the couturier what style of garment they wanted. He would offer his expert advice, but it was ultimately the client who made final decisions regarding designs.[88]

Prices at tailor's shops were high. In 1770 Caracas, for example, some of the products stolen by Coro's rebels were assembled for 1 peso and 2 *reales* a piece.[89] This equaled 10 days of fieldwork for most laborers, which made hiring an outfitter out of reach.[90] Therefore, most workers made their own clothes from imported linen or from cloth created by local artisans.[91]

The clothes worn by residents from societies high and low reflected the intertwined hierarchies of race and class in colonial Coro. As was more common before the advent of capitalism, local landowners and merchants accumulated capital in order to spend it on luxury items, such as clothing. This attire served to signal European élites' race and class. The middling ranks in Coro—mostly of African and/or native American descent—could use their limited acquisitive powers to emulate European landowners and merchants. Clothes, therefore, had the

---

86 Duarte, 228.
87 Ibid., 233.
88 Ibid., 227.
89 Ibid., 228-9.
90 For wages in 18th-century Venezuela, see: Otilia Rosas González, *El tributo indígena en la Provincia de Venezuela* (Caracas: Historiadores SC, 1998), 21
91 Rojas, 235.

power to help these populations ascend the racial hierarchy, from *indio* to mestizo or mulato to pardo. Those with dark skin, however, had little hope of accomplishing this. A further obstacle was that middling groups ran the risk of serious consequences for violating clothing laws, as was seen with de la Peña and her daughters.

But much of the money upper-class whites squandered on garbs was spent before they arrived at the tailor's shop. The reason why lies in the nature of textile manufacturing in Europe.

Flanders

In November of 1787, two officers discovered 22 bales of contraband in Cumarebo, a Caquetío town northwest of the city of Coro. The officials found the goods on a nearby beach, stashed in a crevice between two boulders.[92] The discovery was not uncommon: Illegal trade in European commodities was a ubiquitous feature of life in the region.

The haul from Cumarebo was valued at over 1,050 pesos. Besides four small barrels of gunpowder and two pounds of incense, the 22 bales of contraband were made up of European textiles. Nearly half of these, 452 pesos worth, were manufactured in Flanders.[93]

It is likely that locals acquired these products from Curaçao's merchants. Before being sold in Coro, some of these cloths may have been stored in the Dutch West India Company's (WIC) warehouse on the island. Records from the last quarter of the 18th century usually show just two types of textiles housed there: linen from Flanders and Osnaburg, a heavy coarse cotton made in Scotland and used to clothe enslaved people. During this period, the presence of Flemish linen in the

---

92 "1787: Autos formados con motivo del apresamiento de varios efectos de contrabando, ejecutado por el Guarda Tomás Manuel Barbera en los montes de Pichibrea, costa del mar arriba," Comisos XXXV, AGN, ff. 308-332.
93 Ibid.

WIC warehouse reached a high of 977.5 yards in 1773 and it never fell below 250 yards of fabric.[94] Flemish linen also entered Coro legally, by way of the RCG. In 1779, for example, five company ships exported textiles to the Province of Venezuela, and all of them carried Flemish cloth. All together, these ships brought 2,803 pieces of *presilla*, linen used to make shirts, trousers, and veils, for a value of 23,618 pesos. They also shipped a total of 627 pieces of *bramantes*, a textile made of cotton but threaded with flax, which were worth 6,747 pesos. In addition, the RCG marketed 104 pieces of textiles with line patterns, which held a monetary value of over 2,991 pesos.[95]

Although Flemish linen was coveted in Coro, most people knew little about the place they came from. Today, Flanders spreads across the countries of The Netherlands, France, and Belgium. During most of the 18th century, however, the region was politically divided between France and Austria. Maritime Flanders, in the north, extended from west of Dunkirk to east of Ostend. But most people lived in the interior, which ran south of the coast, extending west of Lille and southeast of Alost. Flemish land is characterized by its low altitude, flat terrain, and natural waterways.[96]

Manufacturing in French Flanders was geared toward the national market, while production on the Austrian side was almost exclusively destined for Spanish America.[97] Flanders had been famous for its textile production since the ancient Roman period. During that time, woolen cloth was shipped throughout the Empire. This trade continued, and by the 12th century,

---

94 "Ingekomen bijlagen van Curaçao, met tafels," WIC 609-16, Nationaal Archief, The Hague.

95 Franklin Mendels signals the Spanish names given to certain forms of Flemish textiles. See: Franklin F. Mendels, *Industrialization and Population Pressure in Eighteenth-Century Flanders* (New York: Arno Press, 1981), 72. Also see Duarte. Data is from: "Expedientes de la Compañía Guipuzcoana de Caracas," Caracas, 934B, AGI, ff. 628-30; "Expedientes de la Compañía Guipuzcoana de Caracas," Caracas 935C, AGI, ff. 30-34, 61-89.

96 Mendels, 51-55.

97 Ibid., 182.

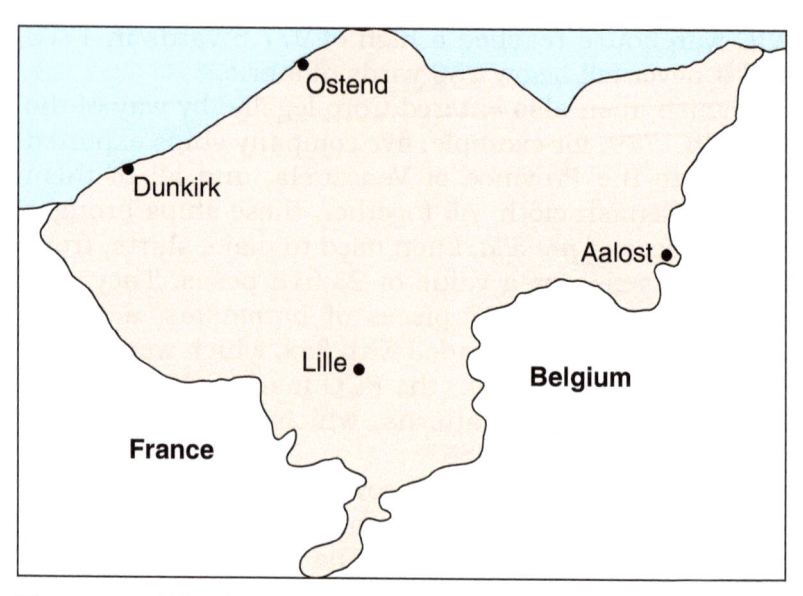

The region of Flanders.

Flanders had become the most industrialized part of Western Europe.

Labor and landholding patterns from the medieval period remained homologous through the mid-19th century. In the maritime zone, large farms produced food for the region and for export. Workers in this area were paid a wage, although they were not forced to purchase commodities for their subsistence. Farmers would sometimes pay for their workers' lodging and board. The vast majority of Flanders's population, though, lived in the sandy interior, where large-scale farming was at a disadvantage, and where artisanal production developed early.[98]

A critical turning point came during the last half of the 17th century. During this time, taxes and rents were increased on Flemish manufacturers, which forced peasants to dedicate more time to fabricating textiles.

---

98 Ibid., 64-82.

It is important to note that this increase in taxes coincided with the growth of Spanish American markets.[99] Small farmers dominated linen production. Big cities such as Ghent and Bruges had been the epicenter of fabrication previously. But as demand for Flemish linen increased, production expanded to the countryside while it deteriorated in the cities. Although Flanders's peasants did grow much of their own food, they could not completely sustain themselves. This was partly because of the poor quality of their land. As a result, many turned to textile making during the medieval period. Peasants then purchased a part of their diet with the cash they earned from selling cloth.[100] The vast majority of small farmers owned the looms and wheels they used to produce fabric. In one region of Flanders, for example, peasants rented only 2.7% of looms in the years 1700-19. Ironically, instead of increasing, this number fell to .4% in 1780-96.[101]

Therefore, most linen fabricators provided their own subsistence, and they owned the tools with which they worked. This limited the industry's growth potential. Cloth exports grew from approximately 120,000 pieces in 1700 to about 175,000 in 1775. This expansion came, not through productive innovation, but through demographic growth and the spread of manufacturing to new towns.[102]

Flanders's proto-industrial system was a complex one that involved thousands of laborers throughout the region. Most flax was sowed commercially in large fields in the northeast, although some small farmers harvested their own.[103] After the flax was planted, it was pulled after maturing at 100 days. It was then bundled

---

99 Christiaan Vandenbroeke, "Proto-industry in Flanders: A Critical Review," in *European Proto-Industrialization*, ed. Sheilagh C. Ogilvie and Markus Cerman (New York: Cambridge University Press, 1996), 111.
100 Ibid., 182.
101 Ibid., 181.
102 Christiaan Vandenbroeke, "Le cas flamand: évolution sociale et comportements démographiques aux XVIIe-XIXe siècles," *Annales* 39:5 (1984): 928.
103 Mendels, 191-2.

Interior with an Old Woman at a Spinning Wheel (1667) by Dutch painter Esaias Boursse (1631-1672).
Public Domain

and placed into a field to dry. Then, the flax was usually taken to the weekly markets that served as an intermediary between peasants and merchants.

Families produced linen part-time as a supplement to subsistence farming. The husband or wife purchased the plants at the market and took them home for processing. The first step was to deseed the flax by beating it. The producers would then ret it to rid it of the components that did not contain fiber. They would then press the plant to remove the stalk's bast. The flax would then be dried and dressed. The last preparatory action was to comb the flax in order to separate its fibers.[104]

Families worked on these threads from home. Production was usually done during the evening and/or in the winter, depending on the household's needs. The mother and her children spun the flax into yarn, although it could sometimes be purchased at local markets. The male head of the household did the weaving. The finished product would usually be taken to the weekly market

---

104 Ibid., 215-17.

and sold to a merchant. Sometimes, however, rural producers would sell their product to a middleman, known as a "kutser." This individual would purchase the linen at a discount, saving the producer a trip to the mart.[105]

This ability to outsource points to the fact that Flemish peasants enjoyed relatively high living standards. A weaver had to work 270 days a year in 1710, but this greatly decreased over the course of the century. Just five years later, required workdays dropped nearly in half, to 140 a year. This number reached 120 days a year in 1740, and an all-time low of 110 days in 1775-80.[106] Health conditions increased as a result of this prosperity, and the region's population ballooned.[107] Inhabitants in the manufacturing zones of the south and east of Flanders increased by as much as 160% during the 18th century.[108]

More people led to more products for Flemish merchants, who were also manufacturers. Big traders usually purchased cloth directly from rural producers. They would then take the merchandise home and bleach it.[109]

Merchants then got the ball rolling on a complex trading system in which they might not see any return for years. They would ship their textiles to a port in Spain (usually Cádiz) under the care of a Spanish recipient. This Iberian partner would then send their Flemish counterpart's goods to the Americas. There they were traded for agricultural commodities. These products would then return to Spain and be reshipped to Flanders. The Flemish merchant would then sell his American product to other European traders. Because of the long wait times

---

105 Ibid., 181-204.
106 Vandenbroeke, "Proto-industry," 113.
107 Herman Van der Wee and Peter D'Haeseleer, "Proto-Industrialization in South-Eastern Flanders: The Mendels Hypothesis and the Rural Linen Industry in the 'Land van Aalst' During the 18th and 19th Centuries," in *Proto-industrialization: Recent Research and New Perspectives in Memory of Franklin Mendels* (Geneva: Droz, 1996), 248.
108 Vandenbroeke, "Le cas flamand," 918.
109 Ibid., 180.

required to see a return on their investment, only the most monied men could become merchants.[110]

The intricate, archaic nature of Flanders's cloth industry was partly responsible for the prohibitive value these textiles held in Coro. The great majority of workers owned their means of production, and they provided an important part of their own subsistence. The growth of manufacturing came not through technological innovation but through the industry's expansion to new villages. Because Flemish fabricators were not wholly dependent on this activity for survival, production was limited to small-scale, part-time peasant laborers. This restricted the number of items that could be fabricated, and this is why prosperous whites seemed to be the only people in Coro who could afford Flemish cloth.

Brittany

Six months after the Coro rebellion, 66-year-old José Manuel de la Cruz Castillo was called to testify about the cache of stolen clothes, jewelry and textiles that he discovered in the sierra. In the aftermath of the insurrection, he led a contingent of militia members and volunteers to arrest suspected rebels and recuperate stolen goods. Among the dozens of items recovered by de la Cruz Castillo's team were "two sheets, from Brittany, already worn-out."[111]

De la Cruz Castillo's mention of Brittany sheets is the only time a cloth's place of origin is included in declarations related to the rebellion. This is fitting because *bretañas* may have been even more celebrated than textiles from Flanders. Brittany cloth was famous in

---

110 Hilda Coppejans-Desmedt, *Bijdrage tot de studie van de gegoede burgerij te Gent in de XVIIIe eeuw: de vorming van een nieuwe social-economische stand ten tijde* (Brussels: Paleis der Academiën, 1952), 27-8.
111 "Expedientes, sublevación de esclavos," ff. 131: "dos Sabanas, de Bretaña, ya usadas."

A map of France and Brittany.

Venezuela for its rippled look and feel, which was unique, and came to be seen as a sign of opulence and panache.

Although the bretaña design was distinctive, their dissemination was wide. There are only four records of contraband cases available from 18th-century Coro that include the place of origin for textiles. Of these four inquiries, three register a shipment of Brittany cloth. Six pieces of this region's linen, valued at 2 pesos apiece, were among the goods confiscated in Tucacas in 1715.[112] More than 70 years later, in 1787, 6¾ yards of bretaña worth 1 peso and 7 reales were seized in El Trapichito. That same year, 13 pieces of Brittany cloth,

---

112 "1715: Autos sobre el comiso hecho en las playas de las Tucacas por el Sargento Mayor Don Luís Francisco de Castro," Comisos II, AGN.

worth 26 pesos, were requisitioned in Pichibrea.[113] But these numbers pale in comparison to those imported by the RCG. In the sample year of 1779, two company ships carried 4,809 pieces of Brittany cloth to Venezuela, which held a value of over 22,000 pesos.[114]

The region of Brittany was as idiosyncratic as the cloth it produced. Located across the English Channel in northwestern France, the people of Brittany descended from Britons, who settled on the land that would later be known as Britain. Partly because of this, Brittany's inhabitants were considered culturally distinct from the rest of France. In addition, most Britons practiced Protestantism in what was officially a Catholic country.[115]

Brittany also set itself apart through its world-renowned textile industry. The earliest records of the activity are from 1430, and from the start linen production was geared almost exclusively to Spanish markets.[116] These dealings would soon include the Americas, and with the conquest and settlement of the region, Brittany's industry flourished. As was the case in Flanders, textile production was adopted because of the poor quality of Brittany's land.[117]

Flax preparation usually started with the import of seeds from Eastern Europe and Zeeland. Peasants bred flax seeds and sold them to merchants at their local markets. These traders would either resell the kernels to foreign dealers or ship them themselves. The trade in flaxseed was massive. In 1750, for example, 12,000 barrels of seeds were imported into Brittany's port of Roscoff.[118] The trade was also lucrative

---

113 "1787: Autos sobre la aprehensión que hizo Don Juan Antonio Barbera, Cabo de Resguardo," Comisos XXXV, AGN; "Autos formados."
114 "Expedientes de la Compañía Guipuzcoana de Caracas."
115 Nancy Locklin, *Women's Work and Identity in Eighteenth-Century Brittany* (Burlington, Vt.: Ashgate Pub., 2007), 9.
116 Jean Martin, *Toiles de Bretagne: la manufacture de Quintin, Uzel et Loudéac, 1670-1850* (Rennes: Presses Universitaires de Rennes, 1998), chap. 1, para. 12-17, https://books.openedition.org/pur/21844.
117 Ibid., chap. 2.
118 Ibid., chap. 5, para. 5.

for merchants. The price per barrel of seed was 35 *livres* at Roscoff, twice as much as it was in the Baltic.[119]

Whereas in Flanders, paid workers produced flax on large farms, peasants in Brittany cultivated the plants themselves. It took a barrel of seed to sow half a hectare. Flax was planted in May and harvested in July, when the stem reached two to five inches high. Small farmers tore the flax out manually in order to make it longer. The plant was then placed in a vat and retted at the base of a fountain on the peasant's property or on the course of a natural, nearby stream of water. The retting process took between one and two weeks. The flax was then taken out of the water and put to dry under sunlight for eight to ten days. Finally, the farmers would take the flax to the local market at Tregor. More often, however, small merchants known as *linotiers* would collect the flax from its cultivators and take them to markets for a commission.[120]

The linotiers played an important part in the industry. They transported flax from Tregor to markets throughout the region. Their horses could carry 60 kilos worth of the plant, which became 10-15 kilos of yarn. These small traders then sold the flax to larger merchants. The linotiers could also serve spinners and weavers with flax so that they did not have to produce it themselves. It was common to see linotiers tour the countryside delivering the product, particularly to widows who were less likely to travel alone to urban markets.[121]

As in Flanders, spinning and weaving were done within the household.[122] In order to spin flax into yarn,

---

119 Ibid., para. 10.
120 Ibid., para. 3-20.
121 Ibid., para. 21-30.
122 Official data on 18th-century weavers is currently unavailable, but records from the first quarter of the nineteenth century shine light on the previous century's labor market. In 1825, there were 5,441 weavers in the three largest linen markets. 3,289 of these workers, or just over 60%, were classified as farmer/weavers, meaning that they were part-time workers who also had access to land. Fewer than 40% of weavers were classified as full-time workers; these are probably those that lived in the urban areas. Although indicative of general patterns, these figures likely underestimate the

the plant was first cleaned to rid it of impurities. Next, the spinners used a *braie* (a homemade tool that resembled a bench) to separate the tow from the woody part of the plant. They would then grind the flax using a tool called a *péseau*, which was made up of two boards that formed at a right angle. Finally, spinners used a *bressage* to comb the plant, which created a string. After these preparatory measures were concluded, the women and children used a spinning wheel, which they owned, to spin the strand into yarn.[123]

Once the plant was spun into thread, the male head of the household wove the yarn into cloth. As was the case in Flanders, weavers owned their own looms. It was often kept in a separate room or in a barn. After woven, the cloth would be taken to the weekly market and sold.[124] But some weavers also had contracts with local merchants. In 1759, for example, François Rabet agreed to manufacture linens for the merchant François Lalleton for four years. He would be paid 4 *sous* per yard of linen produced.[125]

Merchants usually hired small farmers to whiten the cloth after it was purchased. Typical bleachers rented a large house with a barn. These properties contained one hectare of uncultivated terrain on which the cloths were dried. The land also included an area where crops could be harvested in order to feed the tenants.

---

percentage of peasant/weavers in the 18th century. The peak of Brittany's linen industry was in the mid 1770s, and production dropped greatly after 1779. Because the linen industry's expansion was primarily in the countryside, most of those who stopped production after 1779 probably lived in rural areas. Also, the 1825 figures do not include other linen producing regions, which were primarily rural. Nevertheless, the fact that over 60% of weavers in three large linen producing areas were classified as landowners in 1825 indicates that peasants made up the majority of spinners and weavers. Martin, *Toiles*, chap. 6, table 2.

123 Martin, *Toiles*, chap. 5: 31-43

124 Martin, *Toiles*, chap. 6. To become a weaver, he had to join the local guild and serve as an apprentice, which could last 18 months to three years. Apprentices lived with their master. In rural areas, such as Allineuc, employers paid for the apprentices' room and board. In more urbanized areas, such as Quentin, however, families had to pay the master for his services.

125 Ibid.

Bleaching was a drawn out process that required large families to maintain a successful operation. The first step was to put the linens to soak in large wooden vats for three to four weeks. Here, the cloth would soften in a mix of rye, buckwheat flour, and water. The linens were then beaten and placed on a drying rack. This process was repeated for two to three days. Laborers then leached the cloths by placing them in tanks. A bag filled with wood ash was placed on top of the pile, and boiling water was poured over it. This process was repeated between eight and 12 times. Finally, the product was starched.[126]

The textiles were then returned to merchants who stored the goods and hired additional workers to make the final preparations. The first step was to remove the folds from the linen. Laborers then pounded the cloths with wooden mallets. The merchandise was then folded in the shape of an accordion. They were then subject to a softer pounding called a *pilotage*. A highly trained specialist then intervened to turn the folded linen into a piece of 12 layers. The cloth was then ironed around the edges in order to make them sharper. Finally, the layers were pressed to preserve their form. The bretañas were then packaged; first wrapped in gray paper and then covered with a protective cloth. The merchant then labeled the parcel with his name, the name of the launderer, the number and quality of the linens, and the total length of the textiles enveloped. Each bundle weighed between 78 and 100 pounds.[127]

There were four ports in Brittany, but nearly 80% of textiles produced between 1748 and 1788 were shipped out of Saint-Malo. Merchants hired carriers to transport their packages to the port. Once the goods arrived, local authorities inspected them for tax purposes.[128] The vast majority of linen was exported to Cádiz before being shipped to the Americas. For this reason, some merchants from Brittany settled in Andalusia during the 18th century. One hundred French traders were

---

126 Ibid., chap. 7.
127 Ibid.
128 Ibid.

registered as living there in 1771, and about one-fourth of them were from Brittany.[129]

As in the case of Flanders, cloth production in Brittany was done by independent craftspeople, most of whom were peasants who produced textiles part-time. The vast majority of these workers owned their own tools, which were needed for the creation of yarn, the weaving of cloth, and its bleaching. As in Flanders, linen fabrication in Brittany could only increase through demographic growth or the geographical expansion of manufacturing activity. This mode of production was costly and it resulted in the high real and symbolic value of bretañas in Coro.

Devon

Although Coro's revolutionaries were conscious of the connection between European textiles and their labor, not all were thinking of the fact that their very existence was due to the manufacture of these commodities. Most rebels were born in Coro, but their parents and/or grandparents were from West and West Central Africa. The insurgents' forebears had been enslaved and exchanged for European products, most of which were linens. England's South Sea Company (SSC) held a monopoly on the Spanish slave trade for much of the 18th century, and was responsible for bringing many Africans to Coro. They held a factory at Caracas, which imported 5,240 enslaved people between 1715-1739.[130] Some of these individuals were taken to live, work, and die in Coro.

Most of the SSC's textiles were fabricated in Southwestern England, in the region of Devon.[131] The prolific

---

129 Ibid., chap. 2.
130 Colin Palmer, *Human Cargoes: The British Slave Trade to Spanish America, 1700-1739* (Urbana: University of Illinois Press, 1981), 107.
131 Although official figures are lacking, it is clear that Devon was the largest cloth producer for at least the first quarter of the 18th-century. Cloth produced in the Southwest of England accounted for 16% of *everything* exported out of Britain in 1710. See: "How the Regions became Peripheral: A Complex Long-Term Historical Process," by Michael Havinden, Andre Lespagnol, Jean-Pierre Marchand and Stephen Mennell in *Centre and Periphery:*

writer and businessman Daniel Defoe toured Devon in 1724, at the height of the woolen cloth trade. The author of *Robinson Crusoe* gushed over what he saw:

> Devonshire, one entire county, is so full of great towns, and those towns so full of people, and those people so universally employed in trade and manufactures, that not only it cannot be equaled in England, but perhaps not in Europe.[132]

Indeed, Devon was the third most populous area in England, and the country's premier manufacturing hub. Devon's principal port, Exeter, was synonymous with Britain's growing international cloth trade.[133] Defoe recommended that all travelers visit the city's fair: "The serge market held here every week is very well worth a stranger's seeing, and next to the Brigg market at Leeds, in Yorkshire, is the greatest in England."[134]

One regular traveler to Exeter's market was the London merchant Nicolas Cholwell. Although he lived in the capital, Cholwell held estates in Woolston, an aptly named town in the Parish of West Abington and the County of Devon.[135] The trader served markets in the Mediterranean which, along with Holland, were the principal buyers of Devon cloth.[136] Cholwell also sold a significant amount of the product to the SSC. In the same year that Defoe visited Devon, Cholwell vended over £13,114 worth of cloth to the company, the most

---

Brittany and Cornwall & Devon Compared, eds. M.A. Havinden, J. Quéniart, and J. Stanyer (Exeter: University of Exeter Press, 1991), 14.

132 Daniel Defoe, "A Tour Through Great Britain (1724)," in *Early Tours in Devon and Cornwall*, ed. R. Pearse Chope (Devon: David & Charles, 1967), 145-6.

133 W.G. Hoskins, *Industry, Trade and People in Exeter, 1688-1800* (Exeter: University of Exeter, 1968), 16.

134 Defoe, 147.

135 "Will of Nicholas Cholwell, Merchant of London," PROB 11/610/437, The National Archives-Prerogative Court of Canterbury, United Kingdom.

136 Defoe, 147-8. Cholwell was involved in a legal case relating to his trade in the Mediterranean. See: Andrea A. Addobbati, "When Proof is Lacking: A Ship Captain's Oath and Commercial Justice in the Second Half of the Seventeenth Century," *Quaderni Storici* 153 (2016), 727-52.

A map of Britain and Devonshire.

of any merchant that year.[137] It was textiles like these that were used to purchase the ancestors of Coro's rebels.

Commercial cloth production was a profitable enterprise in England throughout the Middle Ages, but it did not begin in Devon until the mid-14th century. During this period, textiles were produced by families and supplied to nearby markets. Wool taken from local sheep provided the raw material needed to spin yarn and weave cloth. A century later, Devon began selling the product overseas, and by 1501-02 Devon textiles accounted for 10% of England's overall exports.[138]

---

[137] "South Sea Company Papers," Manuscripts 25502, British Library, London, England.

[138] Joyce Youings, "The Economic History of Devon, 1300-1700," in *Exeter and its Region*, edited by Frank Barlow (Exeter: University of Exeter), 169.

As was the case in Flanders and Brittany, the vast majority of spinning and weaving was done part-time by peasant families.[139] Because land conditions were not conducive to agriculture, stock raising and manufacturing were done to complement small farming.[140] About 24% of Devon's land was held in common during the 18th century, although it was mostly used to contain livestock.[141]

Despite the preponderance of animal rearing, most of the wool used to make textiles was imported. As manufacturing expanded, local supplies were unable to cover industry needs. Almost all of the wool brought into Devon came from Ireland in the early 18th century. During the peak years of the 1720s, the trade in Irish wool declined, and imports of Irish yarn increased. By 1745, yarn imports were three times that of wool.[142]

Before imported yarn began to predominate, wool was purchased by merchants at Exeter and sold to spinners and weavers at the weekly market. The immense majority of these laborers traveled extensively to get there. Devon's strongest manufacturing region, centered around Tiverton, was 14 miles away.

When raw wool needed to be spun, weavers employed their wives and children. But they usually needed around eight spinners, so they sometimes hired out. Middlemen, known as "yarn jobbers," would arrange the weaver's wool to be spun by nearby laborers.[143] Once the wool was turned into yarn, weavers would use their

---

139 Ibid., 168.
140 Ibid., 165-6.
141 Robin Stanes, "Devon Agriculture in the Mid-Eighteenth Century: The Evidence of the Milles enquires" in *The South-West and the Land*, ed. Michael Ashley Havinden and Celia M. King (Exeter: University of Exeter, 1969), 45; Harold S.A. Fox, "Outfield Cultivation in Devon and Cornwall: A Reinterpretation," in *Husbandry and Marketing in the South-West, 1500-1800*, ed. Michael Havinden (Exeter: University of Exeter Press, 1973), 19-38; David Levine, *Family Formation in an Age of Nascent Capitalism* (New York: Academic Press, 1977), 105.
142 Hoskins, 30-1.
143 Stanley Chapman, ed., *The Devon Cloth Industry in the Eighteenth Century: Sun Fire Office Inventories of Merchants' and Manufacturers' Property, 1726-1770* (Exeter: Devon and Cornwall Record Society, 1978), vii.

own looms to make cloth. From there, merchants would arrange for the product to be finished and dyed.

It is likely that Devon fullers and their families handled the bulk of the finishing processes.[144] In Yorkshire, for example, local lords owned the fulling mills but leased the terrain and the equipment to families. Fulling mills were on arable land and included several homes for immediate and extended kin.[145] Ample space was necessary not only because fulling was a large operation, but also because these families harvested and raised their own food.[146] These workshops were settled near bodies of water because Adam's ale provided the machinery's power. During the late 17th and early 18th centuries, there were dozens of fulling mills sprawled across the county of Devon.[147]

The fulling process itself was an involved one. First, wives and children burled the wooden cloths to remove knots and other impurities. The product was then fulled; massive, water-powered hammers pounded the wet linen. Next, a shearman cut away any loose strands on the fabrics. The cloths were then given to a drawer who repaired any remaining impurities. The drawer then moved the cloth to a pressman, who ironed the textiles using wooden plates.[148] Labor was divided amongst

---

144 Little is known about the finishing processes in Devon, but by using the few details available for Devon and supplementing these with the processes in Yorkshire, a fuller picture emerges.
145 Pat Hudson, *The Genesis of Industrial Capital: A Study of the West Riding Wool Textile Industry, c. 1750-1850* (Cambridge and New York: Cambridge University Press, 1986), 85-9.
146 Ibid., 6. To work as a fuller, men had to serve for seven years as an apprentice for the Guild of Weavers, Fullers, and Shearmen of the City and County of Exeter. Technically, every man who worked in the cloth industry had to belong to this guild, but given the decentralized nature of spinning and weaving, this was impossible to enforce. Although the vast majority of laborers in the cloth industry were weavers and spinners, most Guild members were fullers.
147 Michael Havinden, "The Woollen, Lime, Tanning and Leather-working, and Paper-making Industries, c. 1500-1800," in *Historical Atlas of South-West England*, edited by Roger Kain and William Ravenhill (Exeter: University of Exeter Press, 1999), 339.
148 Hoskins, 56-8.

specialists in Exeter, but rural families did most of the region's fulling.[149]

Once the bulk of the finishing processes were handled, the cloths were returned to merchants who had them dyed. The SSC often arranged for their linens to be colored by professionals in London.[150] In the early 18th century, however, most Devon cloth was dyed and shipped out of Exeter.[151]

Like Flanders and Brittany, textile manufacturing in early 18th-century Devon was done mostly on the household level. Lords owned the land and required some type of payment for its use. Production was a complicated process, involving thousands of craftspeople, the vast majority of whom labored from home, owned their own tools, and worked at their own pace.[152] Most individuals also controlled their own subsistence needs. When British merchants purchased people in Africa with cloth, this was the labor embedded within it.

Conclusion

When we last left María de los Dolores Chirino she had been arrested. She was accused of insurrection, lying to authorities, and stealing clothes and other valuables. After she was apprehended, Chirino was confronted with Don Juan Francisco Santaliz's testimony. He had sworn under oath that he confiscated stolen clothing items from her in the days following the rebellion. When challenged, Chirino responded that she did not mention this in previous interrogations because, as a woman, she was bewildered. Her defender attested, "the

---

149 Celia Fiennes in 1695 observed that all finishing processes are carried out in fulling houses, although she cites only the case at Exeter. See: Celia Fiennes, "Through England on a Side Saddle," in *Early Tours in Devon and Cornwall*, ed. R. Pearse Chope (Devon: David & Charles, 1967), 113-4.
150 See "South Sea Company Papers."
151 Hoskins, 66-8. In 1701, over 83,000 pieces were sent to London from Exeter, although at least three times this amount was produced that year.
152 The link between ownership of tools and the ability to work at one's pace, in juxtaposition to production in the capitalist mode, is made by Levine in *Family Formation*, 1.

confusion and shortsightedness of her sex did not allow her to specify what goods and clothing articles her husband José Leonardo Chirino gave her to put away."[153] In order to avoid prison and/or death, Chirino desperately attempted to exonerate herself by playing to colonial taxonomies regarding femininity.[154]

A few months later, Doña Ana Tellería, the late Joséf de Tellería's sister, pleaded with the court to free Chirino and other enslaved people that her family owned.[155] Tellería insisted that Chirino was innocent. As proof, she referred to two testimonies—including one by a convicted rebel—which corroborated that Chirino was not involved in the insurrection. Tellería added that Chirino had split up with her husband in the days following the uprising, evidenced by the fact that José Leonardo fled Coro and was not found until three months later. As an additional layer of vindication, she concluded that the kind of violence unleashed during the rebellion was "not possible within the feminine breath."[156]

"Therefore," stated Tellería, "María de los Dolores is only part of this summary process for the simple reception of precious objects that Don Francisco Santaliz found."[157] These "precious objects"—European textiles and the clothes they were used to produce—were not hidden somewhere in the mountains because Chirino was innocent. She accepted the merchandise from her husband because she was afraid of him—and for good reason. Chirino handed the objects to Santaliz once he found them. She simply forgot to mention this to Valderrama because "she is afraid that her innocent life is in dan-

---

153 "Expedientes, sublevación de esclavos," ff. 134: "no la permitio la confucion, y cortedad de su sexo expecificar los bienes, y prendas que le dio aguardar Joséf Leonardo Chirino su marido."
154 Beckles, 55-71.
155 Ibid., ff. 159-67.
156 Ibid., ff. 159-60: "no caven en el aliento femenino."
157 Ibid., ff. 160: "Resta pues que María de los Dolores solo parece en el proceso sumariada por la simple receptacion de las alajas que le encontró Dn Fran.co Santaliz."

ger."[158] But unfortunately for Chirino, her family, and her community, Valderrama did not believe her or Tellería. In December of 1796, a year and a half after the rebellion, the Tellería family was ordered to sell Chirino and her children outside of Coro. But Chirino would not make it out of jail alive. The last record of her comes from Joséf de Tellería's will, which reads: "the Mulata María de los Dolores died without being sold."[159] The document adds that she was buried, but that a death certificate was not issued "in order to avoid costs."[160] Chirino, enslaved since birth, separated from her children, and incarcerated for the last months of her life, died in a putrid prison for her possession of "precious objects."

It is unclear whether or not Chirino was actually involved in the insurrection. She may very well have forgotten to tell Valderrama that she held some of Martínez's goods in her possession. Or perhaps Doña Ana Tellería was correct. Maybe Chirino was embarrassed and/or afraid to mention this detail. But it is also possible that Chirino was lying. She could have been an active participant in the rebellion who helped her husband murder Martínez and take his belongings. If Chirino was somehow involved and did not kill Martínez, she was at least eager to receive the merchandise after the deed was done.

Or perhaps the truth lies somewhere in the middle. There appears to have been a spectrum of participation within enslaved people's resistance movements during this period. Some were not involved at all, others were zealous, but it is likely that many—perhaps most— were caught somewhere in the halfway point. Chirino's

---

158 Ibid., ff. 161-2: "incierta del excito del juicio en que teme peligre su vida ynocente."

159 "Testamentaria de Joséph de Tellería, 1798," Archivo Histórico del Estado de Falcón. Coro, Venezuela, ff. 403: "la Mulata María de los Dolores fallecio sin ser vendida."

160 Ibid.: "por evitar costos."

testimony points to this latter scenario as being the most likely, although historians may never know for sure.[161]

Juan Jesús de Lugo was brought to trial in February of 1796, accused of being part of the insurrection. In the minds of authorities, the key to determining his guilt or innocence was to find out what he did with the textiles and clothes of two wealthy white women who lived in the sierra: Doña Concepción Suárez and Doña Ana Vera. Did Lugo steal the merchandise? Or did he hide it to keep it safe?

Suárez and Vera were questioned on the hacienda of Quitaragua because they were too frail to make the trip to Coro. Suárez testified that the insurgents surprised her outside of her estate, and that she felt threatened. Lugo then escorted her back home, although Suárez said that she was unsure of his motives. She did, however, confirm Lugo's account, which claimed that the two worked together to fill one of her hammocks with clothes, textiles, and other valuables. She added that Lugo took this hammock home to hide it from the rebels. But Suárez concluded her sworn statement with a damning pronouncement: The rebels had not assaulted Lugo outside of her home as he had claimed in his declaration.[162]

Vera's attestation contradicted Lugo even more than Suárez's did. The former declared that his testimony was flatly false. It was not true that he arrived at her home in the first hours of the rebellion to help her find her stolen goods. Vera stated that she did not see Lugo until days after the uprising. It was then that he asked Vera for a sack he could use to retrieve her missing merchandise. According to Vera, Lugo added that he had some of her clothes-filled chests hidden at his house as well, and that he would also bring those back.[163]

---

161 This point is taken from the work of Aisha Finch. See: Aisha Finch, *Rethinking Slave Rebellion in Cuba: La Escalera and the Insurgencies of 1841-1844* (Chapel Hill: The University of North Carolina Press, 2015), 141-167.
162 "Expedientes, sublevación de esclavos" ff. 301-2.
163 Ibid.

As was the case with Chirino, Valderrama did not believe Lugo. Over one year later, in February of 1797, he was banished from Venezuela and sent to toil in Puerto Rico.[164] This is the last time he is mentioned in surviving documents.

Chirino and Lugo's stories illustrate the dualities of preciousness and perilousness embedded in European textiles. These served as symbols of race and class in Coro, with the potential to subvert the very order they were meant to cement. Acquiring European cloth and palatial clothes was one of the principal goals for the well-to-do who hoped to procure these treasures by accumulating capital from their plantation operations.

Through stealing and distributing these goods amongst themselves, the insurgents were critiquing this polarity, which was, in essence, Coro's *raison d'être*. The act of redistribution also served as a declaration of what their new republic would be like. Therefore, the stealing of textiles and their reallocation was as significant an ideological proclamation as any reference to the French Revolution.

The centrality of European cloth in the insurrection and its aftermath provides historical evidence for how ideology and materiality underpin one another. The high exchange value of European textiles was largely responsible for their elevated symbolic value in Coro. Their value was high because of the costly nature of linen production in 18th-century Europe.

Thousands of peasants in Flanders, Brittany, and Devon served as the backbone for the textile industry. They grew the raw material used for the cloths, and worked as spinners, weavers, fullers, and a host of other specialty jobs in order to fabricate them. The vast majority of these small farmers manufactured part-time because they were able to provide themselves an appreciable portion of their subsistence. The vast majority of

---

164 "Expediente," ff. 16.

these workers also owned their own tools, giving them the autonomy to work at their own pace and in accordance with their individual needs.

Despite the archaic forms of output employed across the 18th-century Atlantic, these systems still managed an organic relation to one another. Textile production in Flanders and Brittany expanded due to the growth of overseas markets, such as Coro. Coro's plantation economy swelled because of the cheap labor employed in the form of African slaves and their enslaved or legally free descendants. Enslaved Africans were exchanged in their homelands for European commodities, most crucially cloth. And so the Atlantic economy came full circle.

The common belief that the early modern period can be characterized as capitalist runs up against the reality of commodity production during this time.[165] Marx's materialist conception of capitalism's history is helpful here; it explains the historical "stages" of production. Carteblanche, ahistorical uses of the term "capitalism" disguise the qualitative differences between economic modes. Political-economic systems shape the societies in which they operate, yet they can only do so within the framework of their corresponding laws of motion. This is seen again in the manufacturing process of textiles in 18th-century Europe and their consumption patterns in Coro.

But commodities cannot be produced unless they can be circulated. For this, we turn to the joint-stock companies of Europe.

---

[165] This does not mean, however, that these modes of production and the Atlantic system that connected them were not hugely profitable, both quantitatively, and more important, qualitatively. The point made about qualitative significance is taken from Inikori.

Chapter 2

Joint-Stock Company Capital

The textiles that members of Coro's ruling class enjoyed were available thanks to the efforts of three joint-stock companies headquartered in Europe. The Dutch West India Company (WIC), Britain's South Sea Company (SSC), and Spain's Real Compañía Guipuzcoana (RCG) not only provided the region with cloth; they brought Coro's plantation economy into existence. The corporations enslaved thousands of Africans and sent them to toil in the region. What's more, the livestock and sugar estates that the rebels loathed to work on were built because of the economic stimulation that these firms provided. When the insurrectionists killed white élites, burglarized manors, and burned down fields, they were attacking a system of oppression whose core was found an ocean away, in Europe's financial capitals, among wealthy stockholders, blue blood aristocrats, and the continent's leading merchants.

Slavery—that barbarous business that Coro's revolutionaries aimed to destroy—was the product of joint-stock company schemes. In an ironic twist, the 1795 insurrection began its momentum with the passing of a law that was meant to strengthen slavery, rather than eliminate it.

On May 31, 1789, the Spanish Crown issued the "*Real Cédula sobre educación, trato y ocupaciones de los esclavos*"—the Royal Decree on the Education, Treatment and Occupations of Slaves.[166] Influenced by Enlightenment

---

[166] Manuel Lucena Salmoral, "El original de la R.C. instrucción circular sobre la educación, trato y ocupaciones de los esclavos en todos sus dominios

61

humanism, the edict aimed to rein in the excesses associated with slavery without eliminating it. As was the case throughout the hemisphere, rumors soon swirled in Coro that the Real Cédula had abolished slavery. Gossip had it that the local ruling class was holding people in bondage against the wishes of the King.[167] Coro's authorities testified that a mysterious Black wanderer, known as Cocofío, had disseminated the canard, and that José Caridad González continued spreading the rumor after Cocofío died.[168]

If González was fueling speculation, he likely did so within his immediate environment—a neighborhood known as Guinea. Guinea was also the name used in the Atlantic to describe what is known today as West Africa, between the Sahara desert and the Gulf of Guinea. This is the region of the world in which the WIC and the SSC carried out much of their slaving activities. In the city of Coro, however, the term was also used to identify the "free" Black part of town where González lived.

Coro's neighborhood of Guinea lay 30 miles south of the sierra. But despite the distance, the area was linked to the insurrection by curious dances that took place shortly before it was launched. Guinea and its celebrations came to light in the days, weeks, and months that followed the uprising, as baffled officials tried to discern how this conspiracy could have been set in motion right under their noses.

Comandante Don Francisco Jacot was determined to get to the bottom of it. As the head of Caracas's military, the distinguished leader was sent to Coro as soon as word of the uprising reached the capital. His duty

---

de Indias e Islas Filipinas," https://core.ac.uk/download/pdf/58906381.pdf.

167 Abolition rumors were common during the period. See David Patrick Geggus, "Slave Resistance in the Spanish Caribbean in the Mid-1790s," in Gaspar and Geggus (1997): 131-155.

168 "Expediente sobre la insurrección de los negros, zambos y mulatos proyectada en el año 1795 a las inmediaciones de la ciudad de Coro, Provincia de Caracas," 1795, Caracas, 426, AGI, ff. 84-88.

was to oversee military operations in support of local forces, headed by the charlatan Don Mariano Ramírez Valderraín. Jacot brought one theory forward and it was a bombshell. Upon his return to Caracas, after having spent six months in Coro, the Captain submitted a detailed memorial of his time there to Venezuela's Governor Pedro Carbonell. The missive included 29 points that he thought were of the utmost importance. What concerned Jacot the most was the link that he established between González, Coro's rebels, and none other than Ramírez Valderraín himself, Coro's disgraced sheriff.[169]

Jacot suspected Ramírez Valderraín because he uncovered links between him and Coro's Loango community. Jacot's misgivings were on alert the moment he arrived in the region, partly because of "the rudeness with which [Ramírez Valderraín] treated me."[170] His reservations developed further when he noticed that people spoke ill of the Justice Major and of his handling of the crisis.

Jacot admitted that he held this bias against Ramírez Valderraín when he received news that stunned him. It all started when three Loangos—Felipe Guillermo, Domingo Cornelio and Francisco Castro—were apprehended, incarcerated, and accused of being insurgents. But Jacot thought that their apprehension was unjustified because they were militia members. It appears that he saw their incarceration, at that moment, as part of the anti-Black hysteria that gripped Coro in the days following the rebellion. So Jacot ordered that the three men be set free. But he soon regretted his decision because residents began informing him that the three men, particularly Guillermo, were González's confidants.

Jacot ordered that the Loangos be rearrested, and he placed them under the charge of Gabriel Garces, a

---

169 "Sublevacion de los negros de Coro, pieza 3," 1795, Criminales, Letra C, AGN, ff. 70-84.
170 Ibid., ff. 72: "la groseria de que me trataba."

member of the Pardo Militia. Jacot would once again rue his decision when he discovered the three men walking around the prison without chains. This was an intolerable liberty being granted by Garces, and Jacot immediately began questioning the jailer's intentions.

Jacot then toured the city to ask local residents what they thought about Garces. An anonymous member of the Black Militia told him that the jailer was an intimate friend of González. In fact, Garces was dependent on the accused mastermind because he made his living by selling crops that the Loangos harvested in the sierra.

Bringing the conspiracy full circle, Jacot revealed that Garces was a close friend of Ramírez Valderraín. This created just one degree of separation from the infamous sheriff and González, the devilish designer of the May rebellion.

But it was what Jacot reported next that all but confirmed his grievous suspicions. He recounted a conversation he had with Coro's priest, Don Pedro Pérez, in which the clergyman hinted at Ramírez Valderraín's involvement. Pérez told Jacot, "I'm a priest, I've confessed many people, and I cannot say anything else."[171] But despite his purported reservations, he continued:

> suppose that before the uprising, there were some dances or celebrations where people sang some dishonorable little verses, and they danced a thousand obscenities. I remember one that said: a black man with a brand is worth more than the head of a white man: candle up, candle down, take out the machete, cut off the head, the vultures eat, drink the liquor.[172]

---

[171] Ibid., ff. 75: "Yo soy Sacerdote, he confesado a muchas personas, y no puedo hablar mas."

[172] Ibid.: "suponga VMD que antes al levantamiento, se hacían unos Bailes, o Zambras en que se cantaban,, unos versitos muy deshonestos, y se bailaban mil obsenidades: me acuerdo,, de una que dice: mas vale negro con placa, que cabeza de blanco:,,candela arriba, candela abajo, saca la macheta, corta la Caveza, come los Zamuros, beva la Aguardiena."

Pérez claimed that before the rebellion there were festivities in Coro where Black people sang songs, which threatened the lives of local whites. But it was what the priest said next that would stagger and sicken Jacot. The clergyman told him that these songs were sung in the open. The Captain asked if Ramírez Valderraín knew of these dances, to which Pérez responded yes, "because they were public."[173]

Another established gentleman in Coro, Don Nicolás Coronado, confirmed the priest's claims. And the lyrics he provided were even more wicked than those cited above:

> Candle down candle up, the white dies, the black lives: and Josef Leonardo with his gang, together with the blacks in Macanilla, and with a blow from his Royal Palm, the white dies, blacks plant *semilla* [seed]: the white man digs, the black man stays to plant his semilla, those that live will see.[174]

Coronado's statement corroborated that the people of Guinea had advance knowledge of the insurrection. They also knew of Chirino and his designs, and joyously sang about the coming revolution. All this within earshot of those who were supposed to protect the public from ruinations such as these.

Jacot fretted over these diabolical hymns as shocking new revelations poured in. A third official, Don Juan Fermín Emasavel, confirmed to Jacot that the scandalous songs were sung at public gatherings. What's more, Ramírez Valderraín actually attended these parties as

---

173 Ibid.: "porque eran publicos."
174 Ibid.: "Candela abajo candel arriba, muera lo blanco, lo negro viva: y Josef Leonardo con su pandilla, junta los Negros en Macanilla, y con su volezo de Palma Real, muera lo blanco, negro semillan: Blanco cava, negro queda para semillan, quien vivieze lo verán."

an active participant. If true, then the sheriff was either, at worst, an insurgent, or at best, an incompetent fool.[175]

The songs sung by Black people brought to Coro by joint-stock companies could have been the delusions of overwrought white élites, but more evidence ties the tunes to Chirino and the sierra's rebels. In September of 1795, the plantation owner Doña Nicolosa de Acosta described being abused by the insurgents, having her belongings stolen, as well as her home and fields set ablaze. At one point, de Acosta found herself face to face with Chirino, as well as two others. The rebels told her "there should not remain a white man, not even for semilla, that the women would have to accommodate to the new laws, that there was no longer slavery or alcabalas."[176]

De Acosta's account points to the insurgents' use of the word "semilla" to describe both the new society that would be built, and the literal reproduction of African lineage that would take place as a result. Her testimony echoes the usage of "semilla" in the songs sung in Guinea before the insurrection, where the Black semilla was counterposed to the white semilla, which would be eliminated. The landowner's declaration also validates claims made by well off whites that Coro's rebels had

---

[175] See: Pedro A. Gil Rivas, Luis Dovale Prado and Lidia Lusmila Bello, *La insurrección de los negros de la serranía coriana: 10 de mayo de 1795* (Caracas: Ministerio de Educación Cultura y Deportes, 2001); Ramón Aizpurua, "Revolution and Politics in Venezuela and Curaçao, 1797-1800" in *Curaçao in the Age of Revolutions, 1795-1800*, ed. Wim Klooster and Gert Oostindie (Leiden: KITLV Press, 2011), 97-122. Some historians of the 1795 rebellion have questioned the official narrative of González being a mastermind of the insurrection. One historian has suggested that it was unlikely that González, being African-born and the leader of an African-born community, would have conspired with a Venezuelan-born rebel in Chirino, and the largely *criollo* contingent of the sierra. The song quoted above, sung by Guinea-community members in the city, counters these historians' assessments, however, and suggests that perhaps the divisions between *bozal* and *criollo* have been overstated.

[176] "Expediente sobre la insurrección," ff. 291: "no havia de quedar blanco baron, ni para semilla, que las hembras se havian de acomodar a sus nuevas leyes, que ya no havia esclavitud, ni alcabalas."

planned to "marry the white women." Although statements such as these were reflections of planters' worst and most irrational fears, there may be some truth to the claim.

It appears that Coro's rebels planned, not so much to marry white women, but to allow them to live in their new society. It is likely that they were to adopt roles similar to those taken up by Black women.[177] Because white women represented chastity, honor, and beauty in Coro, there may have been a preference for them amongst some insurgents. But they were not considered the same threats as white men, and the insurrectionists probably spared their lives for this reason.

De Acosta returned to her hacienda days later, only to find a shell of her former home. Much of her cane was destroyed. Her clothes, textiles, silverware and tools were gone, and her livestock was decimated. De Acosta was not alone. The landowners Don Josef Antonio Zárraga, Don Jósef de Tellería, and Don Francisco de Manzanos also had their cane fields and homes destroyed, as well as their valuables purloined.

These razed sugar plantations were the product of more than a century of groundwork laid by European joint-stock companies. These firms built the society in which Coro's rebels hoped to plant the semilla of a new civilization, one in which the white ruling class would no longer exist, and where Black workers would govern in its place.

This chapter will inspect three of the principal companies that shaped 18th century Coro: the WIC, the SSC, and the RCG. It shows that the region's revolutionaries were striking against a local political economy that was stubbornly resistant to reform because it was lodged into a much wider political and economic project invested in its immutability. This Atlantic undertaking served disparate interest groups, but ones whose concerns all

---

177 See the next chapter for a discussion of Black women's roles in Africa and in maroon communities in the Americas.

coalesced around the accumulation of capital and the extension of white supremacy.[178]

The Dutch West India Company

If anyone loathed Spain, it was the nobleman merchant, renowned intellectual, and prolific pamphleteer, Willem Usselincx. Born into a pious and moneyed Calvinist bloodline of traders, Usselincx took his already prominent family name to new heights when he became the mastermind behind the prestigious Dutch West India Company (WIC).

Born in Antwerp in 1567, Usselincx was forced to migrate to Middelburg during the Eighty Years War (1568-1648), when the city fell to Spain in 1585. Driven by hatred, as well as an insatiable urge to accumulate wealth, Usselincx proposed creating a joint-stock company that would operate in the Americas. Its goal would be to stake a Dutch Protestant claim into the profitable plundering of Africa and the Americas; to start operations in the Atlantic slave trade and establish colonies in the Western Hemisphere. Usselincx's WIC would fight the blossoming Dutch Republic's archenemy where it hurt them the most—their pockets.[179]

Ironically, the WIC's efforts helped develop Venezuela, one of its rival's burgeoning colonies. The company governed Curaçao, a tiny yet entrepreneurial island, which dominated Coro's economy. Ceded from Spain in 1634, Curaçao lay just 60 miles off the coast of Coro, and the island's merchants illegally imported much of

---

178 My usage of the term "white supremacy" is inspired mostly by the following two works: Charles W. Mills, "Revisionist Ontologies: Theorizing White Supremacy," *Social and Economic Studies* 43: 3 (1994): 105-34; Jemima Pierre, *The Predicament of Blackness: Postcolonial Ghana and the Politics of Race* (Chicago and London: The University of Chicago Press, 2013).

179 Henk Heijer, *De Geschiedenis Van De Wic* (Zutphen: Walburg Pers, 2007), 21; C.R. Boxer, *The Dutch Seaborne Empire, 1600-1800* (London: Hutchinson, 1965); Simon Schama, *The Embarrassment of Riches: An Interpretation of Dutch Culture in the Golden Age* (Berkeley and Los Angeles: The University of California Press, 1988).

the region's agricultural products while they provided it with European goods.

The company also created Coro's African ethos through the steady supply of enslaved people. Some of these individuals were involved in the rebellion, and many more insurgents were descendants of those brought there via WIC activities. The company collapsed four years before the 1795 insurrection, but not before its practices built Coro's plantation system.

The States General of the Netherlands established the WIC in 1621, at the end of their 12-year truce with Spain. The first WIC went bankrupt in 1674. But through coercion and financial manipulations, a second WIC was formed with the first company's dead capital.

The corporation's main interests were in the slave trade and the running of Caribbean colonies. During the 18th century, the WIC owned forts along the coast of West Africa, from which they conducted their trade in enslaved people. In the greater Caribbean, the company ran several plantation and commercial territories, Curaçao being its crown jewel.

Usselincx was one of the first shareholders of the company he envisioned. Investors like him were attracted to the WIC because of its monopoly on the Dutch slave trade, as well as its potential commercial operations in the Americas. These enterprises, they thought, would no doubt bring profits. During the company's initial phase, shareholders were also drawn to the idea of missions to sack Spanish bullion shipments, and were buoyed by major successes in 1628 and 1646. In addition, financiers liked the WIC because investments were considered safe, given that the company was state-sponsored, received government subsidies, and guaranteed regular dividends.[180]

---

180 P.C. Emmer, "The West India Company, 1621-1791: Dutch or Atlantic?" in *Companies and Trade: Essays on Overseas Trading Companies during the Ancien Régime* (Leiden: Leiden University Press, 1981), edited by L. Blussé and F. Gaastra, 76.

The States General's interest in the WIC complemented those of shareholders. Having found great success with its first joint-stock enterprise, the Dutch East India Company (VOC), they considered that the WIC had the potential to plow in similar profits. In addition to serving as an instrument of war against Spain, the States General knew—as Usselincx's works explained—that a joint-stock corporation was needed to pool together enough resources for these Atlantic ventures.

It took several years to raise enough money to begin operations, and the general financial health of the first WIC would vacillate until it went under in 1674. The value of the company's stock was at 115% in 1628 and reached a high of 206% the following year. But in 1633, the stock price fell to 61% of its nominal value, and by 1638, it was consistently selling below this price.[181] That same year, the WIC lost part of its monopoly on Atlantic commerce, but managed to keep exclusive rights to Dutch trade in enslaved people, as well as other profitable commodities, including ammunition and Brazil wood.[182]

This adjustment may have helped the stock value increase in the following years, but by the 1670s, it became clear that the corporation could not continue operating as it had. The WIC's directors concluded that they were losing money because of competition from illegal slave traders in West and West Central Africa. They believed that if they could raise one million guilders, they would be able to strike blows against these interlopers and regain control of the ignominious commerce.[183]

Unable to collect a million guilders, the WIC turned to extortion. The company was dissolved and a second WIC was established using the first corporation's capital. Shareholders were authorized to transfer 15% of their

---

181 J.G. Van Dillen, "Effectenkoersen aan de Amsterdamsche beurs, 1723-1794," *Economisch-Historisch Jaarboek* 17 (1931): 1-46.
182 Emmer, 79.
183 Heijer, 107.

nominal stock from the first company to the second, but they were forced to hand the new firm cash equal to 4% of their holdings. In a similar vein, owners of bonds could have 30% of their investments transferred to the new company if they gave it 8% of their investments in cash. If stakeholders did not agree to these conditions, they would lose their WIC shares.[184] The corporation raised 1.2 million guilders through this scheme, surpassing the one million that they thought they needed to revamp their trade. This was the cash that the second WIC used to begin its operations.[185]

The transition from the first company to the second came with some structural changes to its management. When the firm was inaugurated, it had five regional chambers: Amsterdam, Zeeland, Rotterdam, Northern Quarter (a historical term referring to a northern region of the Province of Holland), and Groningen. Each section elected their leading shareholders as members of the *Heren XIX*, the company's board of directors.[186] With the second WIC, the chambers were kept as they were but the board was reduced to 10.

As before, the company's directors were voted in by the *bewindhebbers*, shareholders who oversaw their province's daily operations. The bewindhebbers were selected by, and amongst, the *hooftparticipaten*—major investors from each chamber. In the Amsterdam chamber, hooftparticipaten were those who had 4,200 florins invested in the company, but those in the other chambers held a minimum of 2,800 florins worth of stock. The *Upperbewindhebber* was William IV of Orange. He technically had final say on matters, but in practice, he was removed from day-to-day dealings.[187]

---

184 Cornelis Goslinga, *The Dutch in the Caribbean and in the Guianas, 1680-1791* (Assen: Van Corcum, 1985), 4.
185 Emmer, 81.
186 Boxer, 48.
187 Heijer, 117.

The bewindhebbers were the backbone of the WIC, and were responsible for all resolutions. In exchange for their service, they received a 10% commission on all dividends. Many bewindhebbers held investments in Atlantic commerce not monopolized by the WIC, and thus used their positions to obtain inside knowledge on market conditions. Importantly, they were also attracted to the position for the prestige that it afforded them.[188]

Paradoxically, the more the WIC accomplished, the more privilege it lost. The company began as a heavily armed monopoly holder of all Dutch trade in the Atlantic. As stated above, the corporation lost part of this monopoly in 1638, but retained its hold on a number of commercial sectors, most significantly the slave trade. The WIC held exclusive rights to Dutch dealings in Africa until 1730, when the trafficking in enslaved people was opened to private concerns. Finally, in 1734, the conglomerate lost its monopoly on the buying and selling of all other African commodities.

From here until the company's demise in 1791, the WIC served as a government administrative entity that operated with the aid of private capital. The last half-century of the WIC's lifespan was dedicated to supporting private Dutch businesses in the Atlantic.[189] Therefore, the WIC's efforts to force open new markets for Dutch economic interests succeeded, and its trading activities became superfluous.

The WIC in Africa

Whether they realized it or not, private Dutch traders relied on the WIC. Key to their slaving activities was the presence of company forts along the coast of West Africa. The Dutch held a dozen fortresses on the Gold Coast from the 17th to the 19th century, which provided

---

188 Ibid.
189 Ibid., 180.

enslaved people to private Dutch merchants looking to complete their cargoes. These strongholds and their personnel also provided traders with provisions and a host of other commodities they could traffic.[190] The copiously armed establishments also furnished security for merchants in case they would require it. They also gave Dutch dealers legitimacy, which was needed to broker with Indigenous peoples.

Like their European rivals, the Dutch traded in enslaved people up and down the West African coast and, to a lesser extent, in East Africa. Taken together, the Gold Coast of Guinea and the Loango Coast of West Central Africa accounted for 54.3% of all enslaved people transported by the WIC between 1700-1738. They also accounted for 47% of enslaved people transported by Dutch merchants during the "free trade" period (1730-1803).[191]

The Low Countries' imperial presence on the Gold Coast began in the late 16th century, when independent traders started conducting business with Indigenous leaders. Some decades later, the WIC became the principal Dutch agent in the region, making major inroads as part of their offensive against Catholic Portuguese claims on the coast.

In 1637, the WIC seized control of the Iberians' fort at Elmina, which then became the center for WIC operations on the entire continent. Elmina was the largest fortress operating on the Gold Coast during the proto-colonial period.[192] It was heavily reinforced, with cannons placed upon a massive, seemingly impenetrable stone wall that surrounded the stronghold.

---

190 Ibid., 124.
191 Johannes Postma, *The Dutch in the Atlantic Slave Trade, 1600-1815* (Cambridge and New York: Cambridge University Press, 1990), 114-121. It is important to note, however, that the latter period is rather imprecise, given that ships with an unknown destination accounted for 33.6% of the records consulted by Postma.
192 The term protocolonial is borrowed from Walter Rodney. See: Walter Rodney, *A History of the Upper Guinea Coast: 1545-1800* (New York: Monthly Review Press, 1970).

Gezicht op Elmina (View of Elmina) (1706)
Nationaal Archief, Public Domain

Half of the WIC's staff in Africa was housed at Elmina. This labor force oscillated between 200-400 people over the company's life span. The Director General was the head of a decision-making council, which included high-ranking military personnel. Most WIC employees were soldiers who, along with sailors and craftsmen, made up four-fifths of all company workers on the continent. The remaining staffers were administrators.[193]

This military gave the WIC leverage when negotiating with Indigenous groups, and allowed the United Provinces to partition a considerable stake in the Gold Coast trade. Before the turn of the 18th century, this commerce consisted of an assortment of African goods, primarily gold, being exchanged for a medley of European and Asian commodities, foremost textiles.

The WIC paid land rent for Elmina. They gave the Asante king six ounces of gold a month, usually in the form of fabrics that were valued at this amount. In exchange for this payment, the Asante assured protection for the

---

193 Ibid., 64.

Dutch and their presence at Elmina. Just as important, this *kostgeld*, as the Dutch called it, guaranteed a steady influx of enslaved people who were regularly brought to the castle in droves.[194]

After the WIC lost its monopoly on the Dutch slave trade, its role was to provide military and commercial support for merchants from The Netherlands. The largest private corporation was the Middelburg Commercial Company (MCC), which accounted for as much as three-fourths of independent Dutch trade in Africa after 1730.[195]

Nowhere was the MCC more active than on the Loango Coast, over 500 miles south of the Gold Coast.[196] The Dutch first ventured into the region in 1593, and were active through the 19th century. The territory, also known as Angola to European traders, was a 460-mile stretch of land along the Western Central African coast, below Cape Lopez and above the Congo River. Loango was also the name of the area's dominant group until the turn of the 18th century.[197]

In the 1660s, the WIC set up a lodge on the Loango Coast, but Indigenous groups forced it closed in 1686.[198] Thereafter, WIC traders, like their European rivals, would have to fend for themselves without the security of castles or lodges. Dutch merchants dealt mostly with independent Indigenous traders, rather than state representatives. In fact, 593 Loango Coast merchants conducted business with the MCC between 1732 and 1797. These were small agents: 85% of them traded an average of less than one enslaved person a year.[199] These middlemen acquired enslaved people from Indigenous

---

194 Larry W. Yarak, *Asante and the Dutch, 1744-1873* (New York: Oxford University Press, 1990), 96-133.
195 Postma, 132. The Zeeland region accounted for over 77% of all African trade during the period, and the MCC was the dominant company.
196 Stacey Jean Muriel Sommerdyk, "Trade and the Merchant Community of the Loango Coast in the Eighteenth Century" (Ph.D. diss.: University of Hull, 2012), 115.
197 Ibid., 37-42.
198 Postma, 60.
199 Sommerdyk, 162.

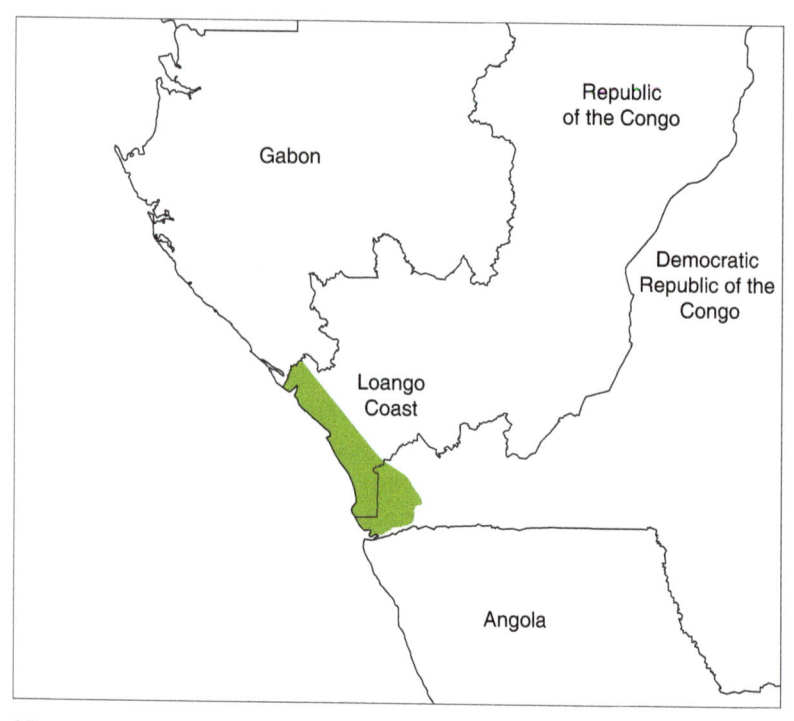

Map of the Loango Coast.

suppliers. Most captives were kidnapped on the coast, although some were brought from the interior, across the Mayombe Rainforest.

Once intermediaries purchased people, they transported them seaboard for sale. The commander of a Dutch vessel would fire a cannon from his ship offshore. The Indigenous merchant and his workers would then guide the captain to an anchoring post. From there, the Loango trader would board the ship to set terms. Once they agreed to details, the Dutch shipmaster touched ground to ensure the availability of enslaved people. While on land, he hired Indigenous laborers to construct a temporary base. It was from this post that business matters were finalized.[200] Dutch slavers spent weeks or

---

200 Sommerdyk, 175-9

months anchored off the coast as new human cargoes were boarded intermittently.

Enslaved people were procured in a more formal manner on the Gold Coast, where the WIC held many forts. Each stronghold would contract a *caboceer*, a local broker. This was usually someone who lived in the small commercial communities that lay outside of the citadel's walls. The caboceer's job was to serve as an interpreter and to collect outstanding debts.

Once they were purchased, enslaved people were kept in an oubliette below the fortress. These dungeons' unsanitary conditions generated much distress, disease and death. Until 1730, the WIC held people in these prisons until their company's ships arrived to pick them up.

After 1730, most enslaved people were procured independently and boarded onto private vessels. But the strongholds still played a key role, as they were almost always the last stop on Dutch slaving voyages. WIC castles provided private merchants food and essential commercial items, including the last human cargoes they needed for the Atlantic crossing.[201]

The Middle Passage was a hazardous voyage, especially heinous for the enslaved people on board. Upon Dutch ships, it was customary to chain men together in the *slavegaaten* or slave hole. Women and children were kept on deck, more easily subject, one could imagine, to the sexual tortures of their transporters. Enslaved people were fed twice a day, at 9 a.m. and 5 p.m., and the men in the slavegaaten were brought on deck regularly for fresh air and exercise. Occasionally, Dutch crews would organize parties where enslaved people would sing, dance and play instruments. These practices were considered essential in order to minimize loss of life. But death was inevitable. Nearly 18% of the enslaved people taken aboard WIC ships died in transit between 1700 and 1739.[202]

---

201 Emmer, 46.
202 Ibid., 240.

Caribbean commerce and the WIC's decline

In the Caribbean, the WIC administered the island entrepôts of St. Eustatius and Curaçao. The company's military presence, as well as its management, made it possible for Dutch marketers to stake claims in the region. The WIC-operated islands also helped the mother country benefit from the supply side of the slave trade, as well as from the procurement of Caribbean produce that was sold in Europe.

Most individuals who survived the Middle Passage with Dutch traffickers ended up in Curaçao. From there, they were sold to planters from places like Coro. In the first 30 years of the 18th century, the WIC brought nearly 20,000 enslaved people to the islet. By the time of the insurrection, the slave trade via Curaçao had declined considerably, although it was still active.[203]

But enslaved people were but one of the many commodities trafficked between Curaçao and Coro. Most trade between the two regions was illegal under Spanish law, so it is difficult to record exactly how much commerce existed between them. In 1778, however, various acts of "free trade" were incorporated in Spain's American colonies, including the Captaincy General of Venezuela.[204] One of the decrees allowed for dealing in particular goods to certain foreign powers. The measures were meant to increase access to enslaved people and specie, two commodities that were in demand, but which Venezuelan landowners struggled to acquire. In 1783, Coro's *Real Hacienda*, the Royal Treasury, began recording recently legalized foreign commerce, which is representative of the overall balance of trade between Coro and Curaçao.

Data on imports from Curaçao is currently available for the years 1788-90 and 1793-94.[205] According to the

---

203 Ibid., 54.
204 Before this time, the Province of Venezuela was under the jurisdiction of Nueva Granada.
205 "1788, pliego 3," Caracas 578, AGI; "1788, pliego 4," Caracas 578, AGI; "1788, pliego 5," Caracas 578, AGI; "1789, pliego 3, Caracas 578, AGI;

free trade laws, only enslaved people and currency could be imported from foreign colonies, but authorities in Coro also recorded other goods.[206]

The vast majority of registered imports were tools used in plantation production. In the five years that are available, Coro's merchants imported 1,501 pesos worth of hoes, 982 pesos worth of machetes, and 672 pesos worth of knives. For some reason, Coro's authorities did not register imports of enslaved people or specie, which were presumably the items that returned to Coro in exchange for the region's exports. The one exception is for 1793, when Coro's authorities noted the importation of 713 pesos worth of silver coin. This coinage amounted to 27% of imports that year, only surpassed by hoes, which accounted for 34.48% of imports.[207]

Data on exports is more complete, and is available for the years 1788-1790 and 1792-94. Most of Coro's sales to the island were in sugar products, the overwhelming majority coming in the form of *panelas*, blocks of raw sugar. In these six years, Coro's merchants shipped 30,893 pesos worth of this product, which accounted for over 50% of all exports to the islet. Cowhides were the second largest product exchanged, amounting to 12,116 pesos or 19.68% of all shipments. This was followed by cows and calves, which were shipped out for 4,784 pesos, or 7.77% of exports. The remaining sales were in Brazil

---

"Libro manual de la Real Caja del Departamento de Coro," Caracas 579, AGI; "1792, pliego 4," Caracas 580, AGI; "1793, pliego 2," Caracas 580, AGI; "Libro manual de las Reales Cajas del Departamento y Ciudad de Coro," Caracas 581, AGI.

206 Eduardo Arcila Farías, *Economía colonial de Venezuela* (México: Fondo de Cultura Económica, 1946), 307-9

207 "1788, pliego 3," Caracas 578, AGI; "1788, pliego 4," Caracas 578, AGI; "1788, pliego 5," Caracas 578, AGI; "1789, pliego 3, Caracas 578, AGI; "Libro manual de la Real Caja del Departamento de Coro," Caracas 579, AGI; "1792, pliego 4," Caracas 580, AGI; "1793, pliego 2," Caracas 580, AGI; "Libro manual de las Reales Cajas del Departamento y Ciudad de Coro," Caracas 581, AGI. It may be pertinent to note that 1793 was an extraordinary year for recorded imports in that the total recorded value of the imports from Curaçao (2,639.5 pesos) is significantly higher than the imports from other years, which saw a low of 339 pesos in 1788 and a high of 779 pesos in 1794.

Goods imported to Coro from Curaçao

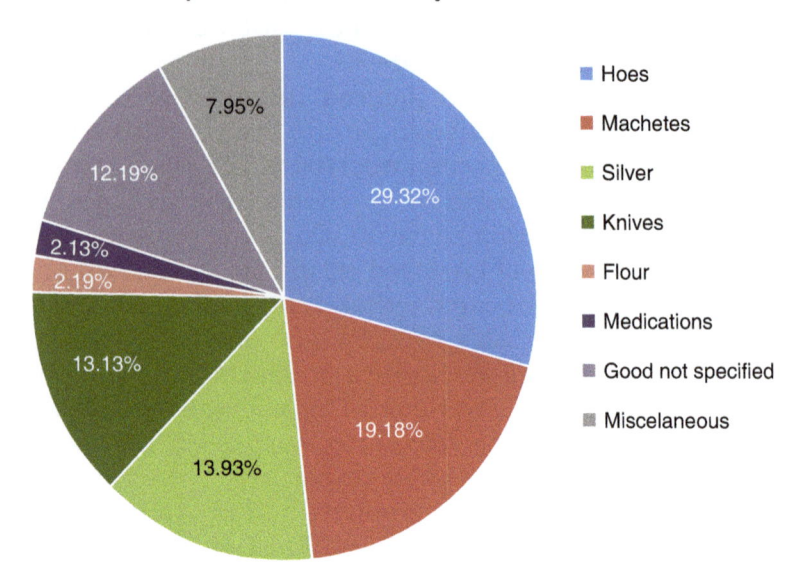

- Hoes: 29.32%
- Machetes: 19.18%
- Silver: 13.93%
- Knives: 13.13%
- Flour: 2.19%
- Medications: 2.13%
- Good not specified: 12.19%
- Miscelaneous: 7.95%

wood, deer, sheep, and goat hides, followed by other miscellaneous animal products, such as fish and turtles.[208]

---

[208] Ibid. There are some problems with these figures. For starters, when the exports documented by Coro's Real Hacienda are compared with those under Curaçao's Day Register, Coro's merchants sometimes arrived on the island with goods that were not reported when they left Coro. For example, in January of 1792, Don Francisco Lucambio was recorded as exporting *panelas* from Coro, but when this shipment was documented in Curaçao, the island's authorities noted that Lucambio had imported animal skins as well.

Another issue with the numbers is that contraband was still common during this period, despite the legalization of some trade. Between January and June of 1792, for example, Curaçao's port of Willemstad registered 18 boats from Coro, but the latter's Real Hacienda recorded only 14 shipments to the island. It is likely that some of these importers were from Curaçao and conducted their trade off Coro's coast because their names do not appear in any of Coro's other accounts.

Despite these defects, the data does detail trade between Coro and Curaçao, and rewrites some aspects of Venezuelan history in the process. *Panelas* were the majority of exports from Coro to Curaçao, showing the dependence that the sierra's sugar plantations had on Curaçao as a market. This evidence counters the common understanding in the historiography that Venezuelan sugar production was geared exclusively towards the domestic market.

These figures also reveal the structure of economic activity in Coro. If cowhide exports are combined with the shipment of the animals themselves, this

Goods exported from Coro to Curaçao

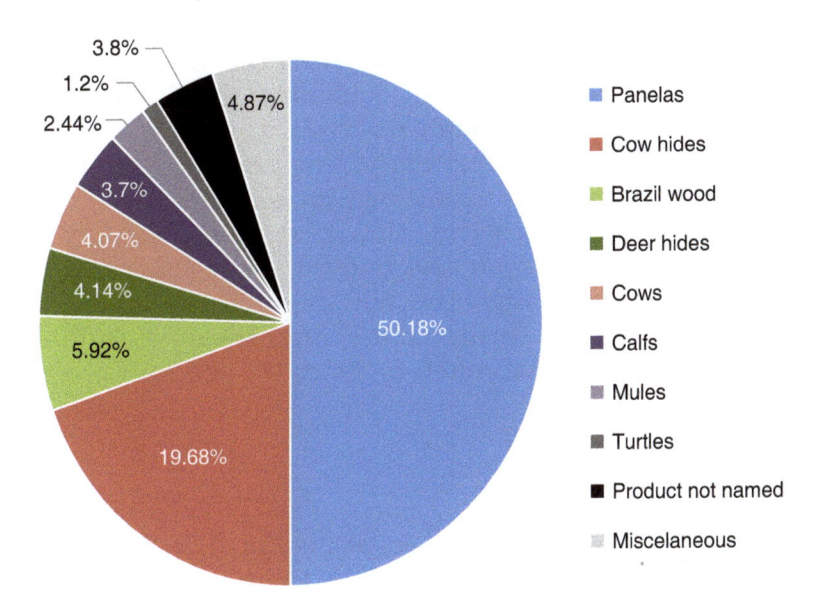

- Panelas — 50.18%
- Cow hides — 19.68%
- Brazil wood — 5.92%
- Deer hides — 4.14%
- Cows — 4.07%
- Calfs — 3.7%
- Mules — 2.44%
- Turtles — 1.2%
- Product not named — 3.8%
- Miscelaneous — 4.87%

Despite its activity in Africa and the Caribbean, the WIC was struggling to stay afloat. In 1785, a commission was appointed to audit the company. They recommended that the corporation borrow 150,000 guilders to pay its outstanding debts. They also suggested that the state subsidize the corporation with 250,000 guilders a year until its charter ended in 1791.[209] The company was disbanded after its contract expired. The States General purchased the corporation's shares at 30% of their nominal value, even though they were trading at 22%.[210] In November of 1792, the United Provinces established

---

totals 17,519.5 pesos or 30.34% of shipments to Curaçao. This makes cattle goods the second-largest area of domestic production for Curaçao's market. Together with sugar, bovine articles accounted for over 84% of all trade to Curaçao. Sugar and cattle products were followed by Brazil wood, which equaled 6%.
209 Goslinga, 599.
210 Heijer, 187.

the Council of the Colonies, which assumed the WIC's administrative duties in Africa and the Caribbean.[211]

Through its 170 years in operation, the WIC molded much of the Atlantic world, including the Coro that imploded in 1795. Through its trade in enslaved Africans, as well as its facilitation of this practice, the WIC was responsible for transporting Coro's rebels and their ancestors to the fates they abhorred. The company's management of Curaçao also buoyed the region's plantation system. Although the WIC no longer existed in 1795, it had already furthered the interests of the Dutch ruling class, and done much to foster the rage of Coro's revolutionaries.

The South Sea Company

The day after he proposed to Parliament that England establish a joint-stock company to trade to the southern seas, Chancellor of the Exchequer Robert Harley was stabbed twice in the chest. On March 8, 1711, a French spy by the name of Marquis de Guiscard knifed the Member of Parliament, just as Harley was leading the charge against him for treason.

Tensions were high between the kingdoms of France and Great Britain, as the two were fighting each other in the War of Spanish Succession (1701-1714). De Guiscard was living in London in exile, plotting to overthrow the French government with the financial and political support of his hosts. But Harley claimed to have stumbled upon damning evidence, which suggested that de Guiscard was a double agent. He accused him of selling secrets to his homeland and, in a fit of fury, de Guiscard stabbed him during initial proceedings.

But Harley survived his wounds. This did wonders for the opportunistic politician's career, as the incident propelled his profile to new heights. The fracas also helped

---

211 Goslinga, 606.

launch the magnetic personality's pet project—the South Sea Company (SSC).

Founded in 1711, the SSC was established as a means to acquire the Spanish Crown's coveted *asiento*. This contract gave signatories the exclusive right to provide enslaved Africans to Spain's American colonies. The asiento was the nonpareil prize of the early modern period, as it gave companies legal access to Spain's massive markets in the Americas—markets that were cut off from all other foreigners.

When the SSC was founded, the war between England, on the one hand, and Spain and France on the other, was expected to end soon. It was assumed that a peace deal between the opposing parties would include handing the rights of the asiento to Great Britain. These hypotheses were proven true when the SSC was officially awarded the covenant in 1713.

Although Harley's company was established to engage in the slave trade, the SSC's purpose was fiscal in nature. When Harley proposed creating the firm, he argued that a corporation like it was needed to restructure England's spiraling debt. These obligations were thought to critically weaken the country militarily. Secretly, the corporation was also envisioned as a proto-Ponzi scheme in which its principal proponents could earn big. This parlous formula caused the 1720 London stock exchange bubble and its bursting, making the SSC responsible for one of the first, and most devastating, stock market crashes ever recorded.

The SSC and the British Crown were able to accomplish their financial goals at the expense of 75,000 Africans who were enslaved and shipped to Spanish America from 1715 to 1739. About 7% of them were sent to Venezuela. Many of these enslaved workers ended up in Coro, and were the ancestors of 1795's revolutionaries.[212]

---

212 Colin A. Palmer, *Human Cargoes: The British Slave Trade to Spanish America, 1700-1739* (Urbana: University of Illinois Press, 1981), 107-110.

The Trade in Enslaved People

The SSC was a latecomer to England's slaving activities, and it benefited from the work of its predecessors. England first established an entity dedicated to the African slave trade in 1660 with the Company of Royal Adventurers Trading to Africa. The corporation would be reorganized and renamed the Royal African Company (RAC) in 1672.[213]

The SSC's foundation was the asiento, and it relied on the RAC to meet their contractual obligations. The asiento stipulated that the SSC was to ship 4,800 *piezas de indias* a year. A pieza de india was a subjective measuring tool used to evaluate the fitness of an enslaved person and their body. Men over 4 feet 10 inches tall were considered a whole "piece" as long as they had no physical "defects." Women and children could be counted as less than one "piece," but this was not always the case.[214]

Out of a sample of 134 SSC ships, it has been found that 55.9% of their captives came from either the Loango Coast or the Gold Coast.[215] The firm did not own many of the vessels it used, but rented most, and commissioned its captain and a crew. The corporation also utilized the RAC to procure enslaved people and to shield their interests. But just as often, the SSC acquired abductees in the same way private traders did. This was by conducting operations on their own, while relying on military support from the RAC, particularly around its forts.

The RAC operated between 15 and 20 settlements during the SSC's lifespan. These structures, varying in size from massive castles to small factories meant to be used temporarily, housed between 200-300 soldiers, sailors, and administrators.[216] By far the most important

---

213 Ibid., 5.
214 Helen Paul, *The South Sea Bubble: An Economic History of its Origins and Consequences* (London and New York: Routledge, 2011), 123.
215 Palmer, 31.
216 Ibid., 23; K.G. Davies, *The Royal African Company* (New York: Octagon Books, 1975), 240.

A photograph of Cape Coast Castle, taken in 2011.
Creative Commons

outpost, and the military and managerial core of the British Empire in Africa, was Cape Coast Castle, located in the town of Fetu on the Gold Coast.

Swedish merchants built Cape Coast Castle, second in size only to the Dutch castle of Elmina, in 1652. Twelve years later, it was sold to the Royal Company of Adventurers, and then inherited by the RAC. Cape Coast Castle was defended by out-works, and surrounded by 14-foot thick walls, which were protected by 74 large guns perched atop. Many more firearms were held inside, alongside living quarters, warehouses, water tanks, and workshops. Under the fortress were underground enclosures used to hold up to 1,000 enslaved people.[217]

British merchants considered the RAC's military establishments essential for trade. This was because relations between Europeans and Africans were fraught

---

217 Davies, 248.

with tension. The kidnapping of white traffickers for ransom, for example, was a common practice during the RAC's tenure. There are also reports of the company's employees taking African agents hostage in order to settle debts. In 1726, Liverpool merchants reported that Africans preferred trading at sea rather than at the forts, because they were liable to receive "abuses" at the latter.[218]

The RAC and the SSC acquired enslaved people in much the same way as Dutch merchants did. The RAC paid 9 marks of gold or £288 as annual rent for the Cape Coast Castle.[219] Indigenous allies would exchange enslaved people to the RAC for European and Asian commodities, particularly textiles. Enslaved individuals were also forced into dungeons below Cape Coast Castle, and other forts, where irons were placed around their feet and/or necks.

The Cape Coast Castle dungeon was notoriously insalubrious, which worried the SSC because they lost money when enslaved people died. In 1718, the citadel's surgeon recommended that enslaved people be given buckets where they could urinate and pass bowels. This suggests that, for decades, enslaved people were forced to sit and stand in their own excrement. Conditions such as these had to be improved, the company directors believed, because some of their human commodities were not even making it to the slave ship. But these instructions were not heeded, and complaints were repeated in 1721 and again the year after.[220]

If they survived their confinement in British forts, enslaved people were purchased by SSC agents. Captain William Eyre, commander of the ship *Russell*, undertook a typical SSC voyage in 1723. The company hired him to sail from London to Cape Coast Castle and then to Jamaica, ensuring that the ship's gunpowder was safely

---

218 Palmer, 34.
219 Davies, 282.
220 Palmer, 42-4.

stored away, and that the ship's gunner was a "sober careful person."[221] Once flanked offshore, Eyre and his crew were to stay on the Gold Coast for no longer than 60 days. At the castle, Eyre was to receive 340 enslaved people from RAC agents. Before loading them onto the *Russell*, he had to first stock the Atlantic voyage's provisions, which were purchased ahead of time from the RAC. These included 14 bushels of salt, 280 chests of corn, 170 pounds of fish and 70 gallons of palm oil.

Enslaved people were to be brought on board 40 at a time, and Eyre was given specific instructions on how to handle his human cargo in order to minimize losses. He and the ship's surgeon were to examine every enslaved individual they took onto the ship, to ensure that "no one wants neither limb or eye, nor that they have any dangerous distemper sore or wound nor be lame sick meagre or refuse."[222] The SSC requested that half of the human cargo be women and the other half men. Six out of seven of these should have been between the ages of 16 and 30. The remaining seventh should have been boys and girls no younger than 10.

It seems that Eyre was asked to take 40 enslaved people at a time because his crew had to wait for the RAC to receive periodic supplies of enslaved people. This indicates that not all 340 individuals were available at once. Eyre was told that if any enslaved person were to die on board during the loading period, the RAC would provide replacements. Once all enslaved people were procured, Eyre would be given a receipt from RAC administrators and was to take a copy with him to Jamaica.

Once en route to the Caribbean island, Eyre was to make a list of everyone on board, alongside physical descriptions of them. If someone was to die on the crossing, he was to "note the numbers at the close of each muster distinguishing their ages and sexes."[223] The cap-

---

221 "Instructions to Captain William Eyres," MS 255567, BL, ff. 10.
222 Ibid., ff. 12.
223 Ibid.

tain was forbidden from throwing any dead overboard without the knowledge of his chief mate and surgeon. He also had to create a certificate of death that included the date and time of passing, and he had to swear an oath that the document was true. If any enslaved person died on the voyage, and they were not documented in this fashion, Eyre was told that he would not be paid.

The commander was instructed "to take particular care that the tobacco beef and spirits laid in for the negroes be expended amongst them and not wasted or embezzled by your men which waste and embezelments has sometimes occasioned great mortality."[224] Eyre was also told to wash the *Russell*'s deck frequently with vinegar, and to "divert" his captives with "musick and play as much as you can."[225] Finally, he was warned to not mix salt water with drinking water. Eyre was asked to create a written account of what practices led to enslaved people's survival or "what may conduce most to their preservation."[226] After the delivery was completed, Eyre was to be compensated four enslaved people for every 104 who survived the Middle Passage.

From Jamaica to Coro

Upon their arrival to Jamaica, captains such as Eyre would transfer custody of enslaved people to SSC agents. The Africans would then go through a "refreshment" period that lasted weeks, but no longer than 30 days. During this time, SSC agents were to improve the physical condition of enslaved people, in order to make them more attractive for purchase. These managers fed their captives twice a day with hearty meals that included beef, fish, rice, bread, yams, fruit, rum and tobacco.

Once enslaved people were deemed ready for sale, they were placed on boats that sent them to Spanish American ports such as Coro. The traders contracted for this

---

224 Ibid., 14.
225 Ibid.
226 Ibid.

job were locals who owned small vessels. They were usually paid a fixed sum per person sold. The captain then traveled to his destination with the provisions that the SSC provided him.[227] This travel through the Americas was almost as deadly as the Middle Passage. Thirteen percent of enslaved people died on these SSC trips from 1720-1725.[228]

The firm probably bought some of Coro's enslaved workers in Curaçao too. The company is known to have purchased a number of enslaved people from Dutch traders on the island, and this was particularly true for Venezuela.[229] In 1730, the SSC's factors in Caracas mentioned that a Mr. Murray Crymble was the "agent and attorney for Curaçao and Coro for some years."[230] This letter is the only document currently available, which references asiento operations in Coro. It indicates that asiento workings in the region were bound to Curaçao. So much so, that the Caracas factors assigned an agent to handle business in the two places as if they were one.

Planters in Spanish America were famously fastidious about the enslaved people they purchased. In 1736, the Caracas factor requested that the people he receive be "the finest deep black" and "without cuts in their faces nor filed teeth."[231] Three years later, an agent in that capital requested that enslaved men be no older than 25, and preferably between 20 and 24 years old. He also asked that the women be from 18 to 20 years old and no older than 22.[232] The SSC also tried to ship enslaved women who were judged to be sexually attractive and "as near as possible be all virgins."[233]

---

227 Palmer, 62.
228 Ibid., 53.
229 Ibid., 59.
230 "Copy of a letter wrote by Cobitt and Berrie Factors at Caracas," SP 36/18/187, The National Archives, Kew, England, ff. 190.
231 Ibid., 62-3.
232 Ibid.
233 Palmer, 75.

The SSC went toe-to-toe with Venezuelan planters throughout their decades of dealings with the province. One problem was the SSC's prices and the allure of contraband. Illegal traders did not have the overhead costs of big companies, so they could sell enslaved individuals for 120 pesos or less, whereas the SSC sold enslaved people for 200 to 300 pesos. This led some plantation owners in Coro to purchase enslaved people next door in Curaçao where they could do so for half the price.

In response to the problem of contraband, the company tried to lower prices of human commodities. In Cuba, the SSC experimented with charging no more than 200 pesos in 1734, although it is unclear how successful the policy was or if it was enacted elsewhere. The corporation also allowed for *indultos*, fines doled out against interlopers whose illegal sales of humans were declared lawful after paying the penalty. Between 1716-19, some 91 enslaved people were brought to Caracas by way of indultos.[234]

Another major issue was that landowners wanted to acquire enslaved people with produce, but the SSC wanted cash. So protracted negotiation between company factors and plantation owners would often ensue. These tussles reached a fever pitch in 1736, when Caracas's treasurer, Don Joseph de Armas, expressed concern that the SSC was becoming unwilling to barter.[235] Armas stated that in 1733, Venezuela traded 6,000 *fanegas* of cacao to the company for enslaved people, but that this number dropped in half the following year. In 1735, Venezuela exchanged a low of 1,000 fanegas for enslaved individuals. (A fanega was equivalent to approximately 1.5 bushels.)[236]

The corporation responded to this issue in a way that favored the colonists. In 1736, the SSC declared that all enslaved people sent to Venezuela would be exchanged

---

234 Palmer, 86.
235 "Certficación numero 3," Caracas 925, AGI.
236 Ibid.

for cacao and other agricultural commodities, what they termed "fruits of the country."[237]

Interests converge

Some Venezuelan cacao wound up in London, and was sipped by stockholders as they dealt SSC shares. London's stock exchange was organized in coffee shops scattered around a neighborhood known as Exchange Alley. Traders would drink chocolate, coffee and tea at these establishments as they swapped shares in publicly owned companies, the most prominent being the SSC. By the time of the 1720 bubble, London's newspapers were publishing stock quotations, which would circulate the Alley's shops.[238]

There were high hopes for the SSC, especially in the beginning. The day before Harley was stabbed, he presented a scheme that would eliminate Great Britain's mounting debt. The kingdom began accruing dues in 1693 once Parliament voted to guarantee all financial obligations that had thereto been personal debt of the King.[239] Harley proposed that part of the government debt be restructured through the formation of a joint-stock company that would trade in the southern seas—Africa and Spanish America.

Government bonds would be converted to stock in the new company. This would save the government millions of pounds in interest payments. Great Britain held £9.47 million in interest arrears when the SSC was established.[240] These bonds were not highly valued, as they were trading at 32 percent.[241] Therefore, the state's

---

237 Palmer, 127.
238 Ibid., 16.
239 John Carswell, *The South Sea Bubble* (Dover, N.H.: Alan Sutton, 1993), 20.
240 Ibid.
241 Richard Dale, *The First Crash: Lessons from the South Sea Bubble* (Princeton and Oxford: Princeton University Press, 2004), 41.

short-term debt was damaging its credit standing, making it more expensive to borrow.[242]

So Harley's plan was to convert the government's floating debt into SSC stock. Great Britain would also set up an annual tax fund of £558,678, which would be transferred to the SSC. With this money, the company could disperse annual dividends to its shareholders.[243] Although the owners of government bonds were forced to convert their assets into SSC stock, they were happy to do so.[244]

Many concerns converged to create the SSC. First and foremost were those of the kingdom of Great Britain. With the expansion of Atlantic warfare in the 17th century, increasing investments were needed for growing militaries and their ships, armor, and weapons.[245] Healthy state finances were required to wage wars. Overseas conflicts were using over a third of government expenditures in 1710, and these could only be met if the country continued borrowing. Another third of state revenues were dedicated to making interest payments, and this figure was projected to rise to 50% of expenses in four years.[246] The collapse of credit markets in Europe following the great frost of 1709 made matters more urgent than ever. This guided the timing of Harley's proposal.[247]

All European powers and traders coveted access to Spanish America's massive market. But these consumers were legally off limits, except for under two isolated circumstances. Exceptions were made for occasions of need during wartime, yet this was too erratic and hazardous a business to depend on. The more significant case—and the

---

242 Ibid., 42.
243 John G. Sperling, *The South Sea Company: An Historical Essay and Bibliographical Finding List* (Cambridge, Mass.: Harvard Graduate School of Business Administration, 1962), 1.
244 Carswell, 45.
245 Paul, 24-35.
246 Dale, 41.
247 Sperling, 3.

most sought after perquisite—was the asiento. The contract was craved because it was known to pour in profits. But just as important, the asiento allowed European governments to dominate their rivals in the war for Atlantic supremacy. With this privilege, states could stake their claim to the largest consumer market in the Americas while closing it off to their competitors. It also gave kingdoms the legal right to confiscate contrabandists' goods, which brought in additional resources and hindered their enemies.

Although traffic in commodities other than enslaved people could be banned in asiento contracts, its beneficiaries always engaged in smuggling. In fact, those vying for the prize factored in contraband opportunities when seeking the agreement. Covenant- holders took advantage of Spanish colonists' desires for European products, which were provided more cheaply via illegal trade. It is safe to assume that most slaving vessels carried a host of black market merchandise.

The SSC's furtive interests were just as important as their publicized ones. Few were aware that the company was the product of a conspiracy that had been underway for some time. Harley's idea actually came from a group of shady speculators: John Blunt, George Caswall, Jacob Sawbridge and Elias Turner. The latter three men were partners in the Sword Blade Company, which received a royal charter in 1691 to manufacture French-style swords.[248] Blunt took control of the company in 1700, and he and his colleagues began using it as a front to illegally dip into public finance operations. These activities were unlawful because the Bank of England held a monopoly on fiscal matters.[249]

The Sword Blade Company and the Bank of England would clash over the right to serve as the kingdom's bank. The drama began when the British government put certain lands up for auction. These properties had

---

248 Dale, 43.
249 Sperling, 5.

been confiscated from Irish Jacobites in the aftermath of the Williamite War (1688-1691). The Sword Blade Company was one of the largest purchasers of these estates, and by the fall of 1702, they had bought £200,000 worth.

To pay for it, the corporation used its privilege to issue stock. Yet these shares were not exchanged for cash, but for army debentures—government debt. The securities stood at 85% on the market but were converted at 100%. Through these manipulations, the Kingdom of Great Britain was able to make a substantial profit, which it used to cancel £200,000 of debt.[250] The Sword Blade directors likely saw gains from this deal too, as they probably possessed some of these bonds.[251]

After this charade was concluded, the Sword Blade Company began issuing mortgages and providing other financial services. The Bank of England responded with legal action against the corporation in 1707, the same year that the Bank had its charter extended. The Bank's new sanction also included language aimed at the Sword Blade Company and its ability to extend credit. The new contract stipulated that conglomerates of more than six individuals were forbidden from issuing loans.[252]

By the following year, the Sword Blade Company was nearly bankrupt. Making matters worse, loyal heirs to the Jacobites, who had their land confiscated, began claiming ownership to the company's property. As a result, the Sword Blade Company's shares fell to 51%.[253] Only a new venture could save the business, as well as the fortunes of Blunt, Caswall, Sawbridge and Turner.

This new venture came in the form of the SSC. It seems that months before Harley proposed the idea of a new joint-stock company, Blunt and Caswall had been in contact with him, and pitched the idea.[254] What *is* known for sure is that

---

250 Carswell, 30.
251 Ibid.
252 Ibid., 31-2.
253 Ibid., 32.
254 Carswell, 35; Dale, 46.

Harley appointed Blunt to draft the SSC's charter, and that Blunt, Caswall and Sawbridge became SSC directors.[255] The Sword Blade Company also managed to finagle its way around the Bank of England's monopoly, and became the SSC's official bank.[256] The Sword Blade Company's underhanded history would weave itself into the tapestry of their new dealings, precipitate the 1720 bubble and its bursting, and ruin the corporation they helped create.

Political interests also conspired to establish the SSC. Harley, a longtime Whig turned Tory, aimed to install a financial interest for his new party, one that could rival the Bank of England and the East India Company, which his former faction dominated. The latter firm's 25-member board included 19 Whigs, while all of the Bank's 24 directors were from the monied party.[257]

Harley got what he wanted. He managed to appoint the SSC's governors and directors, and the vast majority of them were Tories.[258] To seal the matter shut, the new firm's charter stipulated that no governor or director from the Bank of England or the East India Company could serve a similar position for the SSC.[259]

SSC governors and directors were also investors, which drove their association. Governors were required to hold £5,000 of stock, and directors were to hold £3,000. These positions gave them inside information on the corporation, which aided their speculative activities. Governors also received £500 a year as salary, sub-governors received £300, deputy-governors earned £250, and directors received £150. These gentlemen also conducted personal trade with the SSC, even though it was illegal.[260]

Although shareholders were forced to convert their government bonds into SSC stock, they were happy to

---

255 Sperling, 6.
256 Ibid.; Paul, 47.
257 Sperling, 7.
258 Ibid.
259 Ibid., 17.
260 Ibid.

do so. Government debt was not transferable or inheritable, but stock was. An investor could buy and sell shares at their discretion, which was not possible in the case of state bonds.[261] Also, joint-stock companies were few, and investors took advantage of the opportunity to purchase parts of these companies when they could. The SSC's access to yearly payments by the British government made the investment a safe one, and one that guaranteed an annual dividend.[262]

Citizen stockholders were generally motivated by potential returns. The slave trade to Spain's colonies was known to be financially rewarding. Although it never happened, the public was also told that the company would have "security ports" throughout Spanish America, which would facilitate commerce.[263] Another rumor planted was that the SSC was aiming to conquer portions of Spanish territory, which would lead to limitless possibilities for profit.[264] The fact that the Royal Navy protected SSC ships also offered security for their investments.[265]

The Spanish Crown was another interested party. Its many colonies relied on the labor of enslaved African people, and only foreign merchants or governments could supply them. The SSC was formed when England had established itself as the major military power in the Atlantic. The fact that the Royal Navy protected SSC shipments was, again, a form of security for the Spanish Crown. In addition, the RAC—which provided many of the enslaved people that were purchased by the SSC—were the most efficient traders in enslaved people; their voyages were faster and they were capable of providing more captives, per tonnage, than any other entity.[266]

---

261 Paul, 32-3.
262 Ibid., 46.
263 Sperling, 11.
264 Sperling, 9; Paul, 6.
265 Paul, 7.
266 Ibid., 42.

From the standpoint of the Spanish Crown, then, the agreement with the SSC must have been considered a success, even though the company ultimately fell 20,000 bodies short of yielding the 95,000 enslaved people they agreed to ship during the 25-year accord.

If trade had ever been the primary purpose for SSC directors, it ceased being so early on. From 1713 to 1720, the SSC continued converting government debt into shares, and this provided the bulk of the company's capital. As the corporation's valuation moved further and further away from real trade and became more and more dependent on speculation, it created a massive bubble that would burst in 1720. And this nearly brought down the Empire that the SSC was designed to bring up.

The Boom and the Bust

The boom and bust was set in motion in 1719 when the King of Great Britain gave a speech that precipitated the crash. He urged members of the House of Commons to come up with a plan to reorganize all of the country's debt. Blunt proposed that the SSC convert all of the kingdom's existing obligations into company shares.

Despite a counter offer from the Bank of England, the SSC won Parliament's approval to restructure nearly £31 million of government debt. This number accounted for all of the country's liabilities, which were not owned by the Bank of England or the East India Company.[267] The SSC paid £4,156,305 for the privilege of converting the redeemable debt and they agreed to pay a percentage for the irredeemable debt, which could fetch the state an additional £3.4 million.

Therefore, the SSC agreed to pay the government as much as £7.5 million for the privilege to convert state bonds into SSC stock. This scheme was to save Great

---

267 Sperling, 27-8.

Britain £422,499 in annual interest payments until 1727, and £542,499 every year thereafter.[268]

But the SSC had a problem and it was a big one: They did not have £7.5 million. So in order to raise the money, they decided to inflate the price of their stock. In order to entice investors to the scheme, the SSC made stockholders eligible for loans from the company. This credit came with favorable terms, such as installment payments for shares. By the time the 1720 SSC bill passed, the price per share had risen from £130 when the bill was first introduced, to £300 when the first stocks were sold three months later. By this time, the vast majority of the company's capital was held in government debt, and its cash flow came from investments, rather than Atlantic trade.

Therefore, when the SSC lent cash to subscribers, they were advancing them their own money. And when they issued dividends, they were doing the same. The public had not a clue, and stock prices went out of control. On April 1, shares were valued at £302, and this figure ballooned to £950 in July. Stock prices steadily declined before they plummeted in October, falling to £290. This total dropped to £155 two months later.[269]

By this time, the vast majority of shareholders had purchased their stocks at prices well above their nominal value or even their prevailing market price. Fortunes were lost, and the country's political and economic rulers were incensed. An investigation into the company and the bubble brought down a host of MPs charged with taking bribes. The scandal also ruined the company's directors, who were charged hefty fines.

In the aftermath of the crash, Parliament's most important duty was to ensure that the British state was not harmed by this shocking incident.[270] In late December, the legislature passed a resolution declaring that

---

268 Ibid.
269 Ibid., 31.
270 Ibid., 34.

the SSC debt conversions were final. This ensured that the government's burdens would not return to where they were when the swaps commenced in April.

Parliament then softened the blow to investors and rescued the SSC. They cancelled over seven-eighths of the company's government debt, leaving it at £1 million. As part of the deal, the SSC had to pay the government £2 million in cash, plus interest by the summer of 1722. Still burdened with over £7 million of debt, which was owed to the public, Parliament allowed the company to sell part of the annuity the government was contractually required to provide them every year. This move restored the SSC's credit, and allowed them to resume the sale of shares pegged to the £17 million it held in government bonds.[271]

After the bubble burst, and the SSC's financial health was restored, the trade with the Americas, with Venezuela, and with Coro, changed little. The RAC continued to supply a large amount of enslaved people to the Americas on the behalf of the SSC. These shipments halted in 1724, when the SSC began purchasing all commodified people from private traders at Jamaica and Barbados.[272]

The asiento contract with the SSC was terminated five years early due to the War of Jenkins' Ear (1739-1748), which pitted Spain against England in a tit for tat of ship confiscations in the Americas. The Spanish Crown bought out the final years of the agreement for £100,000.[273] Thereafter, the SSC continued managing Great Britain's debt, serving as an intermediary for interest payments between the government and SSC stockholders. This continued for over 100 years until the company was disbanded in 1855.[274]

All in all, the SSC was responsible for ruining the lives of 75,000 people and killing thousands more, while

---

271 Ibid., 44-7.
272 Ibid., 39.
273 Paul, 110-11.
274 Sperling, 48-9.

structuring the plantation economies of places like Coro. The corporation performed these tasks as an instrument designed to further the interests of the British state, as well as mercantile and financial élites. The bubble fiasco, aimed at enlarging the pockets of the company's directors and its key shareholders, resulted in the conversion of most of Great Britain's debt. This allowed the country to grow their military and their Empire, as well as continue its dispossession of non-European peoples.

The Real Compañía Guipuzcoana

Don Joséf de Tellería lived a charmed life before he was murdered. Born into one of Coro's five leading families, he inherited an array of property including 17 enslaved people and El Socorro, the plantation where the 1795 insurrection started. All together, Tellería owned three estates in the sierra and one mansion in the city, as well as 33 enslaved individuals, including María de los Dolores Chirino and her three children.[275]

On top of being a landowner, Tellería was also an active merchant, a dedicated Crown servant, a devout Catholic, and a curious mind. He traded his sugar and plantains to Curaçao, and his mules to Saint-Domingue.[276] Tellería was also a prominent political figure—the former mayor of Coro and the region's deputy for the *Real Consulado de Comercio*, the Royal Chamber of Commerce, at the time of his death. Tellería had his children and slaves baptized and arranged for mass to be held on his plantations. He was also an active reader who kept abreast of the latest in Enlightenment thought from Spain, such as works by the priests Benito Jerónimo Feijoo and Pedro Murillo Velarde.[277]

But Tellería did not become such a sophisticated autocrat by accident. He was the son of José de Tellería,

---

[275] "Testamentaría de Joseph de Tellería, 1798," AHF.
[276] "Cuentas de la Real Hacienda de Coro, 1773-1778," Caracas 575, AGI.
[277] "Testamentaría de Joseph de Tellería."

Coro's factor for the Real Compañía Guipuzcoana (RCG). The elder Tellería was a Basque merchant who migrated to Venezuela during the company's early years.[278] By 1736, just eight years after the RCG was established, Tellería confiscated an illegal shipment of tobacco from Coro.[279] Eight years later, the agent saved enough money to purchase the land where El Socorro was built.[280]

Given that they held a monopoly on the Venezuelan market, the elder Tellería's company played a large part in spurring the 1795 insurrection. The RCG was founded in 1728 through a partnership between the Spanish Crown and Basque merchants already trading in Venezuelan cacao. The firm's activities stimulated plantation production in Coro and provided many of the region's consumer goods. The organization also engaged in a number of other enterprises, including the slave trade. The RCG's efforts took Venezuela from a backwater, dependent on government subsidies, to a Captaincy General and one of Spain's most valuable colonies.[281]

The Spanish Crown spearheaded the RCG's institution because it wanted to support Venezuela's cacao industry, as well as wrestle it away from foreign intruders. Chocolate consumption was growing steadily throughout Europe, from the stock trading alleys of London to the homes of middling families in Madrid. The vast majority of the continent's supply of cacao beans, from which chocolate was produced, came from Venezuela. Despite the fact that cacao came from a Spanish colony, Dutch merchants controlled much of the industry.

---

278 Vicente de Amezaga, *Hombres de la compañía guipuzcoana, Vol. II* (Bilbao: Editorial la Gran Enciclopedia Vasca), 259.
279 "Autos hechos y remitidos por Don José de Tellería, Factor de la Compañía Guipuzcoana en la ciudad de Coro," 1736, AGN.
280 "D. Joseph de Tellería, copia de la Cédula de confirmazion de 36 fanegas de tierra," 1785, AGS.
281 Ronald Dennis Hussey, *The Caracas Company, 1728-1784: A Study in the History of Spanish Monopolistic Trade* (Cambridge: Harvard University Press, 1934), 87.

Spain's failure in Venezuela was a microcosm for its decaying empire. From 1700 to 1728, only five ships had sailed to the colony from Spain, and not a single vessel made the voyage in the years 1706-1721.[282] This was a worrying trend. In 1705, it was estimated that no Spanish ship had sailed to Peru in 10 years, or to New Spain in six years. When they established the RCG, the Spanish Crown was desperate to revitalize its American commerce and they considered Venezuela an untapped goldmine.[283]

The semi-autonomous Basque region of Spain was home to the Province of Guipúzcoa, an area that was trading cacao decades before the RCG's founding. Guipúzcoa was a sovereign state united to the Spanish Crown by a common king. The province held its own assembly and was free from providing men for military service. They also had some autonomy in their commercial affairs.[284] For years, in fact, they tried to have certain duties removed to encourage the cacao trade.

These endeavors failed, and so Guipúzcoa pursued a different strategy. They pitched the idea of a joint-stock company, a partnership between the province, its merchants, and the King of Spain. The cutting-edge corporation would intervene in the foreign-dominated cacao business, while promoting Venezuela's development.[285]

The Spanish Crown approved Guipúzcoa's proposition in 1728.[286] Although the agreement's condition has deteriorated, and not all of its words can be read, the first sentence clearly states that the RCG's primary purpose was to:

> remedy the scarceness of cacao...in this Kingdom...and facilitate to the relief of the public that without having to depend on the judgment of Foreigners that unjustly and

---

282 Ibid., 57.
283 Ibid., 41.
284 Amezaga, 29.
285 Hussey, 52-60.
286 Ibid., 60.

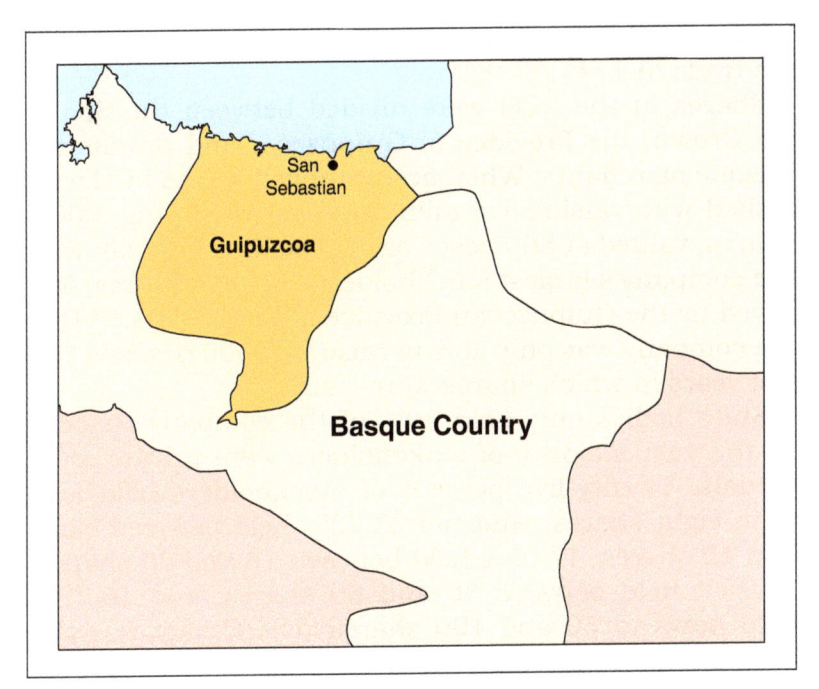

A map of Guipuzcoa and the Basque Country in the 18th century.

fraudulently enjoyed this, and from whose hand the cacao was purchased, this will be managed by Spanish Traders.[287]

The covenant allowed the RCG to send two ships a year to Venezuela, each outfitted with 40 to 50 guns. These vessels could unload their merchandise at either Caracas's port of La Guayra or Puerto Cabello. They could sail directly from Guipuzcoan ports, but had to stop in Cádiz upon their return to pay import duties. At first, the King refused to grant the corporation a monopoly, but this changed just two years later when he agreed to grant no other licenses for Venezuelan commerce. The

---

[287] "Compañia de Caracas: asiento de 1728," Caracas 924, AGI: "remediar la escaséz de cacao...en estos Reynos...y facilitar al comun de España el alivio, de que sin pender de el arbitrio de Estangeros, que indebida, y fraudalentamente le desfrutaban, y por cuya mano se compraba el cacao en ella, le lograsse por la de los Comerciantes Españoles."

RCG was officially awarded exclusive rights to Venezuelan trade in 1741.[288]

Shares in the RCG were divided between the Spanish Crown, the Province of Guipúzcoa, and prominent Basque merchants. When first established, the RCG was tasked with raising 1.5 million pesos by issuing 3,000 shares, valued at 500 pesos each. The King of Spain was the company's largest stockholder, with 200 shares, followed by the Guipuzcoan Province at 100 shares.[289] But the company was only able to raise 750,000 pesos in the five years in which shares were issued.[290]

State bodies only held 20% of the company's stock, so the vast majority of stakeholders were private individuals. Twenty-five percent of stockholders held less than eight shares, whereas 22.73% held between eight and 15 shares, 17.05% held between 15 and 30 shares, 10.23% held between 30 and 50 shares, and 10.79% held between 50 and 100 shares. The Crown was the only entity to hold more than 100 shares.[291] This illustrates that merchants, speculators, landowners and aristocrats owned the bulk of the company.

The RCG's five directors organized trade from San Sebastián until 1751, when the company's seat was moved to Madrid. The Crown appointed the corporation's first directors from a pool of stockholders that held at least 10 shares. Directors earned the lofty salary of 5,000 pesos a year. They were required to meet at least once every five years at a gathering, which could be attended by all stockholders. Investors holding eight or more shares had the right to vote at these assemblies.[292]

---

288 Hussey, 73, 85.
289 José Estornés Lasa, *La Real Compañía Guipuzcoana de navegación de Caracas* (Buenos Aires: Editorial Vasca, 1948), 22; Ramón de Basterra, *Los navíos de la ilustración: Una empresa del siglo XVIII* (Madrid: Ediciones Cultura Hispánica, 1970), 49.
290 Hussey, 65.
291 Montserrat Garate Ojanguren, *La Real Compañía Guipuzcoana de Caracas* (San Sebastián: Grupo Doctor Camino, 1990), 76.
292 Hussey, 64.

Dividends were handed out irregularly during the early life of the RCG until the company made an unprecedented resolution. The first commissions of 20% were paid out in 1735, 1737, 1738, and twice in 1739. Two more were issued in 1741—the first for 26 2/3% and the second for 33 1/3%. The following dividend would be issued ten years later, when 25% was given to shareholders.

A breakthrough occurred in 1752 when the company voted in favor of a radical 100% dividend. This guaranteed a full return on any investment made. The 100% payback would be issued through an annual disbursement of 5%. Thereafter, only a special 10% payout was announced in 1775, with half paid in 1777 and the other half the year after.[293]

Trade and enterprise

But dividends could not be issued if there was no trade. The RCG's directors handled day-to-day operations, arranging the purchase of goods, their shipment to Venezuela, and the return voyages. At their ports in Spain, the company erected storage sheds, which would house one year's worth of merchandise for Venezuela.[294] Sailors were given three months' wages before they set off for the colony and three months' pay before coming back.[295] Between three and six ships departed and returned each year.[296] The company's vessels were given the authority to seize any ships and/or goods engaged in contraband trade as long as they were in Venezuelan waters. The commodities seized were not taxed, and two-thirds of them went to the RCG, while the ship's crew kept the remaining third.[297]

When trips returned via Cádiz, a complex cacao operation would ensue. A government representative

---

293 Ibid., 321.
294 Ibid., 157.
295 Ibid., 82-3.
296 Ibid., 74.
297 Ibid., 62.

would board the ship when it arrived to calculate the duties owed. Muleteers, contracted by the provinces themselves, would then buy the beans at the port and transport them inland, where retailers at the towns' respective markets would purchase them.[298] Cacao sales were done in public auctions twice a year, in March-April, and September-October.[299]

Things changed a bit after the RCG's midcentury reforms. Sales were reduced to once a year, in September-October, and the company expanded its activities beyond Cádiz, Madrid and San Sebastián.[300] Thereafter, the corporation was given permission to supply the beans to Aragón, Asturias, the Basque region, Castille, Galicia, and Navarre. They also were given warehouses at these locations where they could store their products. Sales were made to individuals or to community representatives and it was illegal to purchase cacao in order to resell it.[301]

The Spanish market consumed only half of the cacao that the RCG imported. Spain brought in about 80,000 fanegas of the crop—60,000 of which came from Venezuela—but only consumed 40,000 fanegas a year. The rest was shipped to foreign markets from ports at Cádiz and San Sebastián.

Despite their seemingly unswerving mission, the RCG did experiment with other enterprises. It launched a number of manufacturing ventures designed to buttress their trade with Venezuela. The first and most buoyant was their 1735 takeover of Spain's arms factory at Plasencia. The RCG's acquisition boosted fabrication from 8,000 to 12,000 muskets a year.[302] The corporation's interest in this arrangement was threefold: It could deduct the enterprise's proceeds from the duties they owed the Crown, they would be able to ship part of the product surplus to Venezuela, and their cronies would

---

298 Ibid., 160.
299 Hussey, 157.
300 Ibid.
301 Ibid., 158.
302 Ibid., 169.

earn outstanding salaries by running the operation.[303] The RCG also built a flour mill in Campos, liquor distilleries in Estella and Viana, and began hiring out weavers in Valdenoceda, Rioja, and León. These undertakings were designed to lower the cost of trade and stimulate Spanish industries.[304]

The RCG also dipped into the slave trade. The Spanish Crown issued the company a contract in 1755 to transport 2,000 enslaved people to Venezuela. The firm argued for the contract by stating that the colony had been deprived of enslaved workers since the SSC ceased operations in 1739. The RCG estimated that only 60 enslaved people were legally taken to Venezuela since then.[305] But the company did not come close to fulfilling this agreement. They imported just 310 enslaved people, who were purchased in Curaçao for 45,378 pesos. But before these individuals were resold, 28 of them died and 13 were born. In the end, this accord resulted in 295 people being sold in Venezuela for 62,320 pesos.[306]

Ten years later, the RCG received another asiento to supply the Captaincy General with 2,000 enslaved people. They would purchase these individuals through a factor stationed at Puerto Rico who would receive them from foreign traders. The RCG contracted two outfits to bring enslaved workers to the island. The first was the Weyland Brothers of Great Britain, and the second was an unnamed French merchant. These enterprises were tasked with bringing between 1,000 and 1,100 enslaved people to Puerto Rico. But again the RCG was unable to fulfill their commitment, although they fared better than the first time. By 1769, the RCG had imported 1,013 people under this second agreement, and sold them all in Venezuela.[307]

---

303 Ibid., 74, 267.
304 Ibid., 169.
305 Ibid., 172.
306 Ibid.
307 Ibid., 239-42.

Despite the supposed lack of enslaved workers, cacao yields were soaring in Venezuela. In 1749, the RCG proclaimed that it exported 869,247 fanegas of cacao from the colony in its 17 years of operations. This figure was nearly 25% higher than the 643,215 fanegas of cacao that Venezuela had exported in the previous 30 years. The corporation also claimed that cacao harvests more than doubled between the two periods, from an average of 60 to 130 fanegas.[308]

The RCG's cacao exports continued at a hair above this level until the company lost its monopoly. From 1749 to 1764, Caracas exported over 880,000 fanegas of cacao. Over 500,000 fanegas were shipped to Spain, 300,000 fanegas to Veracruz, 75,000 fanegas to the Canary Islands, and 28,000 fanegas to the Spanish Caribbean islands.[309] But because of the growth of private traders, the RCG lost its monopoly in 1776. The following year, the company exported just 18,000 fanegas of cacao to Veracruz and a paltry 9,691 fanegas to Spain.[310]

The De León Conspiracy, Mixed Results, and the RCG's Downfall

There were troubles even when business was booming, as Venezuelan landowners and RCG factors regularly clashed over payments. These tensions rose to a head in 1749 when the cacao planter and Crown bureaucrat, Juan Francisco de León, led an insurrection against the company. Many planters who thought they were underpaid for their crops shared de León's criticisms of the corporation.

After the rebellion, the RCG conceded that the situation was untenable. They raised the price of cacao to 14 pesos per fanega. But this arrangement required that

---

308 "Certificación del producto de los derechos reales y novenos," Caracas 924, AGI.
309 Hussey, 233-4.
310 Ibid., 270, 316.

the product be traded for the company's goods of the same value. The compact also demanded that the company purchase all the cacao that colonists presented them.[311] Despite these concessions, relations continued to be strained. In 1760, colonists protested that the company was unwilling or unable to exchange cacao for silver coin. They also complained that the RCG's merchandise was overpriced. The firm reacted by slashing the cost of textiles, tools, and oils. They also dropped the requirement that cacao only be purchased with European commodities.

Although they found it difficult to access coin, the company claimed that they had made great strides in providing Venezuela with specie. The RCG reported that from 1750 to 1758, they introduced 2,425,000 silver pesos into Venezuela from Veracruz for an average of 303,125 pesos a year.[312] This amount was higher than the annual average of 253,025 pesos of coin that they imported in 1731-48. The total was also significantly more than the 66,404 pesos a year that were brought to Venezuela in the years 1701-30, before the company began operating.[313]

There is no doubt that the RCG's activities boosted all aspects of the Venezuelan economy, including the industries of Coro. Cacao production more than doubled under the company's watch, sugar yields increased dramatically all over the province, and the number of livestock tripled.[314] In addition, imports of enslaved workers more than doubled.[315] The firm also traded in tobacco and hides, which were both produced in Coro.

---

311 Ibid., 136, 165-7.
312 Ibid., 186.
313 "Certificación del producto."
314 "Manifiesto, que con incontestables hechos prueba los grandes beneficios, que ha producido el establecimiento de la Real Compañia Guipuzcoana de Caracas," Caracas 924, AGI, ff. 13-14.
315 "Certificación del producto."

From 1749 to 1764, the RCG exported 88,000 *arrobas* of tobacco and over 177,000 hides to Spain.[316]

The RCG also shaped the region with its military, which was dedicated to combating contraband. In 1760, the company had 15 ships at its disposal, 10 of which patrolled the Venezuelan coast at any given time. Taken together, this naval guard came equipped with 518 men, 92 cannons and 86 guns.[317] The RCG used this force to confiscate goods being illegally trafficked. There was a pattern to these requisitions: One or two RCG vessels would approach the contrabandist's boat and open fire, to which the interlopers would return shots as they retreated to land or escaped via canoe. RCG soldiers would then take possession of the smuggled goods and return to shore.[318] The corporation also had 12 land patrols of 10-12 men each that would frequent contraband hotbeds.[319]

This clampdown was extremely successful. During the first 10 years of the company's operations, the Dutch share in Venezuelan cacao declined sharply from over 43% to 10%.[320] Although this figure would climb to an average of 30% from 1741-1755, this was still significantly lower than previous Dutch portions of the trade.[321]

Therefore, the RCG managed to reduce smuggling—significantly during certain periods—but it never fully disappeared. In 1779, a Dutch traveler to Curaçao, J.H. Hering, wrote that trade to Venezuela was hazardous because of Spanish coast guards. He added that only small shipments could be carried to Venezuela, but that Spaniards went to Curaçao more often. There, they could "get a pretty good price for their merchandise."[322]

---

316 Hussey, 234.
317 Ibid., 148.
318 Ibid., 149.
319 Hussey, 233.
320 Calculated from Klooster, 228-9. The year 1733 is missing from Klooster's figures.
321 Ibid. Post-1755 records for cacao exports are currently unavailable.
322 J.H. Hering, *Beschrijving van het eiland Curaçao* (Amsterdam: S. Emmering, 1969), 59: "vry goeden prys voor hunne Koopwaaren maken."

Hering was right. In 1757, the RCG reported that Dutch merchants could sell their manufactures 35% cheaper than they could.[323] Traders from Curaçao would also buy cacao for two to four times higher than the RCG. When the firm purchased the crop for 8-12 pesos a fanega, Dutch merchants would pay 24-26 pesos if they were purchased in Venezuela and 30-32 pesos if acquired in Curaçao.[324] Between 1769-1771, at least 34 ships left Curaçao for the Captaincy General of Venezuela. These carried over 194,500 pesos worth of merchandise and returned with over 229,275 pesos in coin, 16,196 fanegas of cacao, and 144,855 hides.[325]

Contraband finally took its toll and the RCG's powers were eroded. After decades of complaints from Venezuelan plantation owners, the burgeoning ideals of liberalized trade gave through in 1777 when the RCG lost its monopoly. By this time, the company's surplus had climbed to 1.8 million pesos. After war broke out in 1779, however, the company's fortunes declined, and by 1781 their assets had fallen to 1.17 million pesos. By 1783, it had decreased by half, reaching 559,096 pesos.

Two years later, the RCG announced its liquidation. But a new joint-stock company was created in its place. The Philippine Company continued providing Venezuela with goods, 2,000 tons a year, in fact. The new entity was also granted a 25-year monopoly on trade with the Philippines. Although the RCG was dissolved, stockholders were encouraged to transfer their holdings to the new company. Venezuela's "free trade" period began in 1780 and started in Coro three years later.[326]

Because of the RCG's efforts—in tandem with those of the WIC and the SSC—Venezuela went from an underdeveloped and overlooked slab of land in Spain's vast Empire to a Captaincy General and the pride of the

---

323 Hussey, 181.
324 Ibid., 273.
325 Ibid., 249.
326 Ibid., 273-93.

mother country, the *madre patria*.[327] The company ballooned the province's cacao output, struck debilitating blows against contrabandists, and stimulated the trade in enslaved people, while experimenting with the practice itself. These pursuits shaped Coro's political economy—the one its revolutionaries gave their lives to depose.

Conclusion

Ramírez Valderraín testified before Venezuela's Royal Audience in Caracas two days after Jacot submitted his censure. He was sent from Coro for a deposition that lasted seven days. The first question the dishonored sheriff faced was whether he had—at any point—suspected that an insurrection was coming, to which he flatly answered "no."[328] The next five queries concerned the dances and seditious songs that so concerned Jacot and the Crown Regent.

At first, the sheriff steadfastly denied that unusual celebrations took place in the days leading to the rebellion. The judge followed up by asking if anyone talked about "abusive" songs being sung. The ill-reputed leader responded that nothing was mentioned, "before verifying the uprising."[329] He added:

that the black Luangos [sic] or [Black people] from Curaçao that inhabit the City's neighborhood of Guinea have always been accustomed to have a dance out in the open, on the eve of a holiday once they retire from their labors in the countryside, turning on their candles if there is no moon, but always asking for a license from the Justicia Mayores, who put up guards when it seems appropriate, and even attending [the dance] in order to avoid whatever disorder because there are no other amusements in that city. People from all classes

---

327 Ibid., 87.
328 "Sublevacion de los negros de Coro, pieza 3," 1795, Criminales, Letra C, AGN, ff. 86.
329 Ibid.: "antes de verificarse la sublevacion."

attend until the middle of the night, the principal men and women of the town. The blacks are accustomed to singing at these dances in a language that you cannot understand.[330]

Ramírez Valderraín then declared that he remembered hearing "*Pa'* semilla" chanted at the dances, but that he did not grasp its significance. He said that it was not until after the uprising when he understood that the expression meant, "the Blacks wanted to extend their generation through the white women."[331]

Ramírez Valderraín's overall point was that there was no way that he or any other official could have known about the insurrection in advance. He conceded that there were dances before the rebellion, but he insisted that these were common in Guinea and that songs were often sung. But the Justicia Mayor also testified that he later realized that he had heard threats in the hymns. Therefore, he contradicted himself by inadvertently revealing that there were, in fact, signs that indicated that an insurgency was afoot.

It is not clear what, if anything, came out of Jacot's accusations and Ramírez Valderraín's defense. But the quarrel points to a likely conspiracy between the largely creole population of the sierra and the mostly African-born community of Guinea. Jacot's testimony, when paired with de Acosta's, indicates that semilla was a fundamental allegory used by both groups.

---

330 Ibid.: "que los negros luangos o de Curaçao que habitan en un Barrio de la Ciudad llamado Guinea han acostumbrado siempre quando se retiran de las labors del campo en las visperas de fiesta poner baile al raso encendiendo su candelada, sino hay Luna, pero pidiendo siempre licencia a los Justicias Mayores que la han dado como el declar.te poniendo Guardia quando le ha parecido oportuno, y aun asistiendo el mismo a fin de evitar qualquiera desorden porque no hay otra diversión en aquella ciu.d suelen concurrir a ellas presionar de todas clases, y hasta la hora de recogerse que en la media noches, los hombres y señoras principales del Pueblo: Que en estos bailes acostumbrar los negros cantan en lengua que no se entiende sus canciones."

331 Ibid.: "los Negros trataban de extender su generacion en las Blancas."

It is unlikely, however, that the sheriff was involved in the insurrection. Jacot's claims were used to accentuate his primary contention that Ramírez Valderraín had failed in his responsibilities. It seems that Jacot's charges of treason were the product of a personal rivalry between the two military men.

After the rebellion was crushed—and long after Cocofío, González, and Chirino were dead—various landowners received reparations from the Crown. These were handed out to aid the plantation proprietors for damages they suffered during the insurrection. De Acosta was awarded a pension of 300 pesos a year. Don Josef Antonio Zárraga's heir, Doña Felipa Caro, as well as her son and her daughter, were given 600 pesos a year until the girl was married. Caro was also awarded a 2,000 peso dowry for her daughter's future wedding. Doña María Josefa Rosillo, the widow of Don Joséf de Tellería, as well as her two daughters and three sons, were endowed with a payment of 100 pesos a year each. The male Tellerías would receive this money until they were 25 years old, and the women would collect it until their deaths or until they were married. The Tellería family was also made exempt from taxes and their debts were placed on hold until the boys were old enough to pay them.[332]

Coro's hacienda owners—*hacendados*—received reparations because they were part of an institution that was too big to fail. They were one element of an Atlantic machination that connected functionaries, traders and landowners in the Americas to agents and military officials in Africa, and to merchants, speculators, and aristocrats in Europe. This political economy was able to function because imperial states supported, and often guaranteed, the assets of affluent whites. Upper-class merchants and financiers, in turn, backed these empires.

---

332 "Expediente."

Nowhere was this public/private partnership more crystallized than in the organization of European joint-stock companies. The WIC was created as a weapon against their Spanish rivals at the end of a truce. It was envisioned as a means to further Dutch commercial interests in Africa and the Americas, and to do so by force if necessary. The British government formed the SSC largely out of their need to restructure the country's spiraling debt, but also to grant their merchants access to Spanish American markets. The Province of Guipúzcoa and the Spanish Crown created the RCG to tap into, and further develop, Venezuela's cacao industry, which had been dominated by foreign rivals, particularly the Dutch.

Although merchants and shareholders were hoping to make profits from their investments, they had other reasons to finance these operations as well. Bankrolling the WIC was a safe venture because it had government backing, which made it a viable alternative to hoarding money. Many SSC investors were attracted to the company for speculative reasons, in order to turn a large profit in a matter of weeks. Before the 1749 de León rebellion, RCG funders were enticed by the promise of high returns on what was essentially a new colonial enterprise, in the restructuring of Venezuela's economy. Later, investors became interested because they were guaranteed their money back after the announcement of a 100% dividend.

Regardless of their motives, the WIC, SSC, and RCG created 18th-century Coro and the region's racialized political economy. Operating for more than a century and a half, the WIC established a Dutch stronghold in the trade of enslaved workers, furthered Dutch interests in this commerce, and opened the door for private merchants to take over. The company also took Curaçao—sitting just 60 miles from Coro—from a Spanish cattle depot to the premier trading station of the greater Caribbean. Through acquiring the asiento, the SSC furthered Great Britain's share in the slave trade to places like Coro, and helped propel the Empire's hegemony over

Atlantic waters. Through its monopoly of the Venezuelan market and its chief product cacao, the RCG awakened Coro's dormant economy. To bring things full circle, the RCG worked with the SSC to import enslaved people as it cracked down on Dutch interlopers who were under WIC protection. These activities ballooned Coro's Black population and created its plantation economy.

When Coro's revolutionaries expressed their desire to eliminate white men, they did so because their world was based on the dominance of white capital and the denigration of Black workers.[333] But this system was unable to eliminate the communitarian political and economic practices that stood in the way of its designs—neither in Coro, nor in the rebels' homelands.

---

[333] The term "white capital" is borrowed by W.E.B. DuBois. See: W.E.B. Du Bois, *Black Reconstruction in America, 1860-1880* (New York: The Free Press, 1935).

Chapter 3

The People

Isolated at the base of Mount Abantos, in the vast wilderness of the Sierra de Guadarrama, the prodigious El Escorial complex is both an oddity and a marvel. Featuring a royal palace, a church, a monastery, a college, and a library, the cluster was built in the late 16th century, at the height of Spain's Empire, with the riches that flowed in from the blood of African and native American people.

El Escorial was decorated with gold pillars, altars, and frames, and its ceilings were covered with murals painted by Spain and Italy's finest artists. Suffice it to say, the palace and its grounds were exclusive territory, reserved for Spain's royal family, visiting dignitaries, and the European world's leading luminaries.

Add to this list José Caridad González. Born in the Loango Coast and enslaved as a child, González fled slavery in Curaçao to live free in Coro. Enterprising and astute, he rose to a position of prominence in Venezuela and was known as the leader of Coro's sizable and established Loango community. Four years before the 1795 insurrection, González took the long journey to El Escorial in an effort to meet with King Carlos IV (1788-1808). On October 29, 1791, González accomplished his lofty goal.

González's appointment with the King of Spain uncloaked the hidden source behind the insurgents' revolutionary ideologies. The Loango leader met with Carlos IV to ask for land. And it's easy to understand why. Land

A photograph of the Monastery of San Lorenzo de El Escorial, taken in 2019.
Creative Commons

was the source of wealth in colonial society. But for most rebels, it was not necessarily about riches.

As was the case with nearly all of Coro's revolutionists, the Loangos were born in West and West Central Africa or one or two generations removed from the continent. In their native lands, they practiced collective husbandry in towns where work was divided evenly among community members, and where the products of these labors were distributed equitably. Customs such as these anchored the Loangos' notions of "equality," making the intellectual idea, newly fashionable in the 18th century, as tangible as it was abstract.

The Loangos recreated some of these practices in Coro, but ran into trouble doing so. As González explained to the King, a prominent plantation owner was evicting them from their land. Don Juan Antonio Zárraga was doing so because he claimed that the territory belonged to him, and that the Loangos were squatting.

In a damning resolution for Zárraga and the local authorities who supported him, the king ruled in González's favor. He granted the Loango leader a Royal Order for the property. According to the document, the Loangos had been "peacefully enjoying the land in the territory of Santa María."[334] This was until Luis de Rojas, the head of Coro's Black Militia, sold the grounds to Zárraga. The order established that the sale was void because Rojas was never the rightful owner. It concluded that González and the Loangos should be provided "justice" without "complaints," "trouble nor any form of harassment."[335]

Carlos IV, rey de España (1789), by Spanish painter Francisco Goya (1746-1828)
Public Domain

But the Loangos never received their due. Even with the legal certification they acquired, they continued to be forced off their land. And the struggle over Santa María de La Chapa continued, culminating in the 1795 uprising.[336]

The legal tussle between Zárraga and González, which was unresolved up until the insurrection, was just the latest incident in a quarrel that went back decades. It was first recorded 20 years before he received the Royal Order. In December of 1771, Zárraga successfully pressured Coro's authorities to forcibly remove the

---

334 "Real Orden," October 29, 1792, Caracas, 375, AGI: "disfrutando pacificamente un terreno en el territorio de S.ta Maria."
335 Ibid.: "quejas...molestia ni vejacion alguna."
336 "Expediente sobre la insurrección de los negros, zambos y mulatos proyectada en el año 1795 a las inmediaciones de la ciudad de Coro, Provincia de Caracas," 1795, Caracas, 426, AGI, ff. 372: "qualesquiera papeles que existtan en la Secrettaria de Capittania General, y escribanias de Govierno, relattivos al pleitto que sobre tierras seguian los negros luangos de Coro con la casa de Don Juan Antonio Zárraga."

Loangos from the land, and they were sent to live four miles away in Macuquita. Coro's Black Militia leader, Rojas, stated that because the Loango community was so large, and their numbers proliferating, he was authorized "to little by little and with the best convenience send them to royal land in the said Macuquita, which are more comfortable, more extensive lands, and with better waters."[337]

But the process was far from convenient and comfortable; some Loangos were jailed for refusing to move. Two men from one arrested party, Francisco Bartolo and Juan Antonio Curazao, testified before a Caracas Tribunal on April 13, 1772. They said that they had been incarcerated for five months, simply for cultivating their land. Bartolo and Curazao added, "in this settlement there is a neighbor named Don Juan Antonio Zárraga that causes us great harm, for he has even taken water away from us and tries to remove us from the entire possession."[338] The prisoners also claimed that Zárraga paid Rojas to "remove us from there."[339]

A few years later, Zárraga discussed his side of the story. He stated, "the free blacks from Curazao hoped to disrupt me on the same lands, without any foundation except for me having added them to these with pious spirits that they could stay there if destiny allowed it."[340] Zárraga's claim that he had allowed the Loangos to stay on his land, but that they were now "disrupting" him

---

337 Cited in: Miguel Acosta Saignes, *Vida de los esclavos negros en Venezuela* (La Habana: Casa de las Americas, 1978), 196: "a que podríamos poco a poco y con la mejor comodidad irlos mandando a la tierra realenga de dicho Macuquita, que son tierras más cómodas, más extensas y con mejores aguas."

338 Cited in: Rivas, Dovale Prado and Bello, 90: "en este sitio se halla un vecino nombrado don Juan Antonio Zárraga que nos sirve de grande perjuicio, pues hasta el agua nos la ha quitado y nos procura desapropiar de toda la posesión."

339 Ibid.: "desapropiarnos de allí."

340 Ibid., 89: "pretendieron perturbarme en las mismas tierras los negros libertos venidos de Curazao, sin otro fundamento que el de haberlos agregado en ellas con piadoso ánimo de que pudiesen mantenerse entre sí si se les daba dicho destino."

may have been somewhat true. As Rojas stated above, the Loango community was growing continuously, as families grew and newcomers arrived from Curaçao. So on the one hand, it seems likely that the Loangos squatted on the lands of La Chapa, understanding that it was unclaimed. As the community grew and as their fields expanded, their presence became a nuisance for their neighbor—a plantation owner who may have been looking to grow himself. But on the other hand, Zárraga did not have any legal claim to the land. If he had, it would have been recorded and King Carlos IV would have ruled in his favor. It seems that Zárraga was just as guilty of squatting as the Loangos were.

The struggle for La Chapa mirrored the Loangos' other major battle of the period: their fight for arms. Just eight months before the insurrection, Coro's Justicia Mayor, Mariano Ramírez Valderraín, divided the city's Black Militia into two. The original one, headed by Rosas, comprised mainly formerly enslaved, Curaçaoan-born refugees. But because there were so many migrants from Curaçao, the sheriff agreed to form a second Black company, one exclusively made up of the African-born Loangos. González and his Loango contingent were eager to form a militia so they could increase their power, while separating themselves from Rojas.[341]

The African-born Loangos wanted González to be the captain of the newly formed militia, but they found trouble appointing him. When González's confidants— Juan Felipe Guillermo, Juan Bernardo, and Domingo José Nicolás—made the petition for a new militia, Ramírez Valderraín told them that González could not be appointed because he was in Caracas. The militia head had to be present to receive an official title.

The sheriff then named someone else as captain. He also claimed that he sent the men's petition to the Captain General in Caracas, but that he responded by

---

341 "Sublevacion de los negros de Coro, pieza 3," 1795, Criminales, Letra C, AGN, ff. 96-100.

naming Nicolás Soco as *teniente* (second in charge) and Juan Domingo Rojas commander. Juan Domingo was a close friend of Juan Luiz Rojas (no known relation) and a member of his militia. Soco and the Loangos returned to the sheriff insisting that González be named their captain.[342]

Ramírez Valderraín was sympathetic to the Loangos' position, and he sent a missive along with the three Loangos to Caracas for an appeal. Guillermo, Bernardo, and Nicolás set off for the capital and returned in January or February of 1795, accompanied by González. It is unclear if González officially took charge of the militia in the eyes of Coro's authorities. However, he was named as the unit's Captain on the 46-man roll that the new company handed Coro's officials.[343]

Conflicts such as these led some Loangos to participate in the planning and execution of the rebellion. Juan Francisco Año Nuevo, who worked on the Socorro plantation, was accused of planning the insurrection alongside Chirino at the home of Juan Bernardo Chiquito.[344] On the first night of the uprising, Juan Luis Martín, an African-born Loango who lived and worked on Doña Nicolosa Acosta's estate, was identified as the rebel who lit the match that burned de Acosta's door down. Martín was also one of the two rebel spies apprehended at Caujarao on the night of May 11. Martín and another Loango, known only as Flores, were allegedly sent to the city to inform González of the revolutionaries' whereabouts.[345]

The mysterious "Flores" may have actually been Juan Francisco Flor, an established member of González's militia. Five months after the rebellion, local white landowner Don Juan Echave reported that Martín was a

---

[342] Ibid.
[343] "Expediente," ff. 47-9.
[344] "Expedientes, sublevacion de esclavos en la sierra de Coro, 1795," 1795, Judiciales, A16-C54-D11183, ANH, ff. 87-95.
[345] "Sublevacion," ff. 120-25.

corporal in González's Loango militia and that he filled the same role with Chirino's insurgents in the sierra. But Martín was not listed as a member of the Loango force.[346] However, the first corporal of González's group was Juan Francisco Flor.[347] It seems that Echave confused Martín for Flor, and that Flor is the "Flores" identified as one of the Loango spies.

Hours after their comrades freed Martín and Flor, González and 21 other Loangos arrived at the sheriff's house asking for guns. They got there after 2 p.m. on May 11, soon after the Justicia Mayor received word that there was an uprising underway. But by the time the Loangos arrived, 40 white and pardo volunteers were positioned outside of his home.[348]

The Loangos appeared with seven or eight guns and requested more for those who were not carrying. The sheriff immediately became suspicious and advised the *ayudante* (aide de camp) of the Pardo Militia, Gabriel Garces, to confiscate the guns they were holding. The sheriff later testified that González said "he would obey but in a disgusted way."[349] Ramírez Valderraín then told González, "he did not doubt his loyalty to the King, as well as that of his companions, but because they are saying that the rebels are black, it would be best if Caridad, and his companions would enter and stay in a room."[350] Coro's military head then escorted the men to a bedroom, although he viewed the detention as a precaution rather than a necessity. The Loangos stayed in the room through the following day.[351]

---

346 "Expediente," 315-17.
347 Ibid., ff. 47-9.
348 "Expedientes, sublevación de esclavos," ff. 111-16.
349 Ibid., 113: "dijo obedecia pero con un modo que significaba repugnancia."
350 Ibid.: "aunque no dudaba de su fidelidad, y la de sus companyeros al Rey, pero como les decía que los levantados eran negros, convenia que el mismo Caridad, y dichos sus companyeros entrasen y se estuviesen en un quarto que esta en el mismo."
351 Ibid.

But the men resisted their confinement. Five months after the insurrection, Captain Nicolás Antonio de Nava, Don Juan de la Paz and the enslaved woman, Gabriela Sárraga, all testified that the Loangos had repeatedly tried to escape. Nava stated that González often asked to be let go, "saying that he and his twenty two other armed blacks were obliged to capture the rebels."[352] At one point, González tried to force his way through the bedroom door. As it was kept shut by guards on the other side, González began "sticking his hands through the door trying to force it open, which was responded with going after a gun and requiring him to contain himself because if he did not, his hands would be removed."[353] Nava added that González replied to the threat by taking away his hands and turning silent. The Captain continued that González "did not speak again and he was bothered when he heard a cannon which was shot at the insurgents."[354]

Hours later, the rebel force experienced their first defeat at the hands of Coro's ragtag royal army. After the decisive battle of the early morning of May 12, 24 rebels were captured and escorted to the city center. According to Ramírez Valderraín, every prisoner testified the following:

> that the black Luango Josef de la Caridad Gonzales who was in court, and in that capital [Caracas], attempting to become the captain of those of his nation; had inspired a thousand errors in the slaves and free blacks, telling them that for the first he had brought a royal document in which your Highness had declared them free, and that the leading subjects of the city were hiding it; and to the

---

352 "Expediente," ff. 309: "diciendo que el con sus veinte y dos negros armados, se obligava a prender a todos los sublevados."
353 Ibid.: "meditendo manos a la puerta pretendio forsarla a cuya accion abocandole un Trabuco y requeriendole a que se contubiera pues de lo contrario se quitava."
354 Ibid.: "no bolvio a hablar, y amostaso al oir un cañonaso que tiro a los amotinados."

second ones that in aiding his designs for the uprising of the slaves, it was they that would rule afterwards in a republic. There is universal truth that the zambo Leonardo, head of the main insurrection of the hills, that he would be the one that started the movement in the countryside, and when he came down to the city he would find aid with the people that followed Josef Caridad Gonzales.[355]

Coro's authorities claimed that González had been telling Black people that the 1789 law regarding the treatment of enslaved people was actually a pronouncement of emancipation. They added that González was stating that he had proof in his hands—that the King of Spain himself had given him a copy of the decree during his 1791 visit.

Immediately after the 24 insurgents were barbarously beheaded, the sheriff ordered that González and the Loangos be transferred from his home to Coro's jail. The sheriff later stated that González was killed during the move when he "ran off with two of his closest people."[356] In September of 1795, an administrator in Coro, Don Gerónimo Tinoco, provided more details of what transpired:

in front of the jail's door where the beheaded blacks were, horrified without a doubt of that spectacle, Caridad

---

355 "Expedientes, sublevación de esclavos," ff. 6-7: "que el negro Luango Josef de la Caridad Gonzales que estubo en la corte, y en esa capital, pretendiendo la capitania de los de su nacion; havia inspirado mil errores a los escablos y negros libres, diciendoles, que para los primeros havia traido real cédula en que su Magestad los daba por libres, y que los sugetos principales de esta ciudad se la havian ocultado; y a los segundos que auxiliando sus designios a la sublevacion con los esclabos, serian los que mandasen despues en republica; en cuyo concierto es constancia universal entro en el zambo Leonardo cabesa de motin principal en la serrania, este havia de ser el que diese el primer movimiento en los campos y quando vajase a la ciudad havia de auxiliarse de la gente que siguiera al Josef Caridad Gonzales."
356 Ibid., ff. 7-8: "emprendio fuga con dos de los mas inmediatos de su gente."

escaped from the guards, and he ran away with two others who were followed by some members of the same guards, and they were killed by blows from sabres and lances at a short distance.[357]

González and his two comrades died a horrific death on the afternoon of May 12, 1795. Not only did they suffer through stabs, but their murder took place in the middle of a macabre exhibition of 24 headless bodies. González's struggle for land and arms ended with his grisly demise, as well as that of his fellows.

The lives and deaths of Coro's Loangos point to the significance that land, autonomy, and sovereignty had for the region's revolutionaries. Their desire for equality and independence was pitted against dehumanizing labor, dependency, and white supremacy. Being denied the grounds they felt they had a right to use, some Loangos responded by forming a militia and fomenting a revolution. Once supreme power was seized, a new republic would be established, presumably similar to the semi-autonomous communities they had already created.

The Loango *Cumbés*

On July 7, 1775, the Dutch West India Company (WIC) compiled a catalogue of enslaved people who escaped Curaçao in the prior 30 years. It was part of the corporation's effort to request reparations from the Spanish Crown, who granted these individuals refuge in an attempt to stymie their Dutch rivals. The island's masters reported that they had lost 537 people during this period. According to the company, every single one of them settled in Coro.

These individuals were known as Loangos in their new home, whether or not they descended from the African

---

357 Ibid.: "al frente de la puerta de la carcel donde estaban tendidos los negros degollados horroisado sin duda de aquel espectaculo se escape de la escolta Charidad, y se puso en fuga con otros dos a quienes siguieron algunos de la misma escolta, y fueron muertos a sablasos y lansasos a poco trecho."

coastline that bore the name. The Loangos were a tight-knit community who resided in the city of Coro and in the semi-autonomous *cumbés* of the sierra. Cumbé was the term used in Venezuela to describe a settlement removed from governmental and church control, although most cumbés were made up of maroons— formerly enslaved Black people who illegally escaped their condition.

Maroon communities existed throughout the Americas since the first enslaved Africans were brought to the hemisphere. Settlements were found in North, Central, and South America, as well as in the Caribbean islands. Anywhere between a handful of individuals to thousands inhabited these communes. Some communities lasted just a few days or weeks, while others existed for decades. Some collectives, like the Loangos, were legally sanctioned. But most existed while being constantly under attack by white colonists. Despite these differences, there were striking similarities among maroon communities. Social, economic and political structures were consistent across time and place—and the Loango cumbés were no exception.[358]

According to the WIC's register, about 18 people fled slavery in Curaçao every year to live free in Coro. As was the case in most maroon communities throughout the Americas, the vast majority were men. Women accounted for 79 of those who absconded during the period in question, meaning that an average of two or three women left Curaçao for Coro every year. Most took their children with them. Twenty-two youngsters fled the island for the province during this time, and 16 of them came with their mothers. Only six boys journeyed to Coro alone.

It is clear that most of the men who settled in Coro were married and had children. But taken together, women

---

358 Alvin O. Thompson, *Flight to Freedom: African Runaways and Maroons in the Americas* (Jamaica, Barbados, Trinidad and Tobago: University of West Indies Press, 2006).

Refugees from Curaçao to Coro, 1745-1774

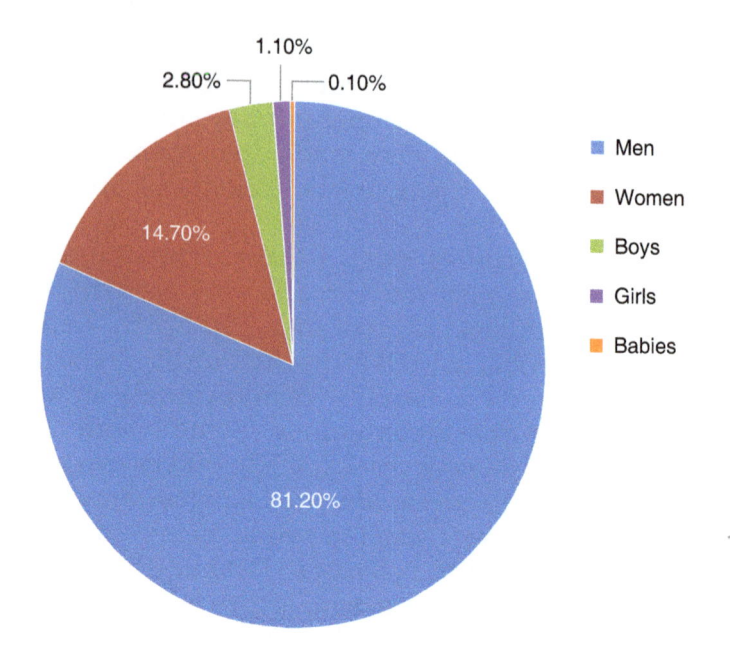

- Men: 81.20%
- Women: 14.70%
- Boys: 2.80%
- Girls: 1.10%
- Babies: 0.10%

(14.71%) and children (4.1%) made up only 18.81% of refugees while adult men represented over 81%.[359] This means that most Loango men married Black women born in Venezuela. González's wife, for example, Jossefa Leonarda de Piña, was born in Coro, was legally free, and racially and sexually classified as mulata.[360]

Hundreds of people lived in the Loango polities. One month after the rebellion, Coro's *ayuntamiento*—the city council—reported that they "make up a large and united congregation in homes and *conucos*, with a sort of species of economy and republics."[361] The ayuntamiento

---

[359] "Lyst der slaaven," WIC, 610, July 7, 1775, NAN, ff. 292-301. Women may have been less likely to abscond because their family obligations were comparatively higher than they were for men.

[360] "Expediente," ff. 301-3.

[361] "Informe por el Ayuntamiento de Coro," April 21, 1796, Caracas, 95, AGI: "componen una numerosa congresacion unida en casas y conucos, con una especie de economia y republicas."

added that the cumbés were "formidable" entities due to the fact that the Loangos "demand contributions from their individuals which are deposited in the community's coffers for their public needs."[362]

Each home in the cumbé kept its own garden where families planted vegetables, such as cabbage and corn, and raised farm animals.[363] This is how households ate. In documentation referring to Loango lands in the sierra, the plural form of the term conuco (conucos) is usually applied, suggesting that each cumbé had more than one conuco. This followed the pattern practiced on most of Coro's plantations where enslaved individuals were assigned a plot of land from which they were expected to feed themselves and their families. This practice was also typical in the Loangos' homelands.

Evidence of agricultural customs on the Loango cumbés is scattered, but a fuller picture emerges when studying the practices of other maroon communes in the Americas. In Venezuela, in September of 1794, Miguel Guacamayo was apprehended after spending ten years in a cumbé.[364] After he was caught, Guacamayo discussed the importance of land in his settlement, stating that whoever refused to work the terrain "was expelled from the community."[365] The Trelawny maroons of Jamaica cultivated about 100 acres of land where they grew plantains, cassava, corn, and cash crops such as tobacco and cacao. The women did most of the cultivating, and the men raised livestock.[366] Agriculture was the primary economic

---

362 Ibid.: "exigen desus indibiduos contribucion q ban depositando en las cajas de comunidad para sus urgencias publicas."

363 "Sublevacion," ff. 94-5.

364 Federico Brito Figueroa, *El problema de tierra y esclavos en la historia de Venezuela* (Caracas: Universidad Central de Venezuela, 1985), 238-9. It is not clear at this moment whether or not Guacamayo lived in one of the cumbés of the Valles of Tuy or Aragua, outside of Caracas, or in Yaracuy, outside of Puerto Cabello.

365 Ibid., 240: "era expulsado de la comunidad."

366 Casey Robinson, *The Fighting Maroons of Jamaica* (Jamaica: William Collins and Sangster, 1969), 68-9.

activity of Brazil's Palmares, and the most important crop was corn, which was grown on plantations twice a year. After the corn-cultivating season, community members would take two weeks off for rest.[367]

Resources were distributed equitably in maroon communities. Living in close quarters, and in precarious situations, unity was of uppermost importance for these groups. Concord was achieved by ensuring that everyone had their needs met. There was also little incentive to accumulate wealth because of the small amount of assets available, as well as the need to regularly uproot and move settlements.[368] In Cuba, most maroon communities held land in common, and it is safe to assume that distribution was handled in a like fashion.[369] This is demonstrated in the name of Cuba's largest maroon community, *Todos Tenemos*—we all have what we need.

Members of the Loango cumbés also hunted, fished, and gathered wild fruits and vegetables. Coro's ayuntamiento stated that Loango children "are dedicated to gathering wild fruit."[370] Picking wild plants was a common practice in maroon settlements.[371] Hunting and fishing were key sources of food for members of the Palmares community, as were manufacturing activities such as weaving baskets, hats, fans and molding ceramic bowls.[372] Men from maroon communities in Jamaica would hunt birds and catch turtles, and men and women would also make salt for local consumption.[373]

---

367 Edison Carneiro, *O quilombo dos Palmares* (Rio de Janeiro: Editora Civilização Brasileira, 1966), 28.
368 Thompson, 212.
369 Gabino La Rosa Corzo, *Runaway Slave Settlements in Cuba: Resistance and Repression* (Chapel Hill and London: The University of North Carolina Press, 2003), 231-2.
370 "Informe": "los dedican a coger frutas libertres."
371 Thompson, 249.
372 Carneiro, 2.
373 Mavis C. Campbell, *The Maroons of Jamaica, 1655-1796: A History of Resistance, Collaboration & Betrayal* (Trenton, N.J.: Africa World Press, 1990), 47.

Agricultural goods—including cash crops such as sugar, tobacco, and cacao—were consumed within Loango communities, but some were also bartered at local markets. In their 1772 testimony, Bartolo and Curazao stated that they cultivated the land of La Chapa "with fruits not just for the supplicants but also for the neighbors of that city."[374] Also, as was seen in the last chapter, the Pardo Militia member Gabriel Garces worked with the Loangos to trade some of the crops they harvested.[375]

Although Loango settlements in Coro were communalist, there did exist a hierarchy of command where leaders held some material advantages over others.[376] After he obtained a Royal Order, González rose to a position of power in his community. On the second of June, just a few weeks after the rebellion, Captain Don Manuel de Carrera wrote that González "turned into a petty king or cacique of slaves who gave him gifts, attended to him, and had considered him so much that without hardship or industry he lived idly and comfortably in the placid tranquility of the city."[377] Carrera added that González's followers were like his "tributaries."[378]

This portrayal is likely an exaggeration. Ramírez Valderraín also indicated that González held a special position within his community, but one that depended on the services he could provide his group. The sheriff stated that González's wife, de Piña, had come to him the year before the insurrection to complain that the Loangos were failing to provide for her while González

---

374 Rivas, Dovale Prado, and Bello, 90: "con frutos no solo para los suplicantes sino tambien para los vecinos de aquella ciudad."
375 Carneiro, 2; Thompson, 258.
376 As Thompson points out, this is typical of most, if not all, communalist societies. See: Thompson, 211.
377 "Expediente," ff. 89: "se conbirtio tambien en un regulo o casique de esclavos que lo regalavan, attendian y conciceravan tantto que sin fatiga, ni industria vivia ocioso y comodamente en la apacible tranquilidad de la ciudad."
378 Ibid., ff. 90.

was away.[379] But the sheriff asserted that the Loangos had come to this agreement with González and de Peña because the former was in "Madrid and Caracas on errands in the interest of the same black Luangos."[380] Therefore, the service provided by his followers was in exchange for his assistance to the larger community.

Bonds were further forged through language and custom. The ayuntamiento testified that the Loangos "conserve their foreign dialect in the language with such precision that you cannot discern the new arrivals from the naturals even though they are different."[381] Ramírez Valderraín also made this point in the months following the rebellion when he declared, "I did not understand their conversations because they were in their Dutch or Guinea language."[382]

Like maroon settlements elsewhere, the Loangos practiced an open-door policy. Practically anyone who wanted to join the community was welcome. They may even have accepted Venezuelan-born slaves who had escaped their masters.[383]

The Loango cumbés also had their own legal system. Coro's ayuntamiento testified that they "use an authority which they gave themselves and that they find convenient for their government, arresting, awarding, and punishing in accordance with their barbaric and despotic caprice."[384] Like maroon communities elsewhere, the Loango settlements had rules, regulations, honors,

---

379 "Sublevación," ff. 101-3.
380 Ibid.: "Madrid y Caracas en dilig.s interasantes a los mismos negros Luangos."
381 "Informe": "ellos conservan su estrangero dialecto en el idioma con tanta exactitud q noze disiernen los advene_sos de los naturales aun que sean distintos."
382 "Expediente," ff. 302: "no entendia sus combersaciones por que era en su idioma olandés, o de Guinea."
383 Acosta Saignes, 196.
384 "Informe": "disponen con autoridad conferida por simismos lo q conciben combeniente a su goverio, prendiendo, apremiando, y castigando segun su barbaro y despotico capricho."

and penalties based on established laws.[385] But the Loangos were not completely removed from the influences of colonial authorities. As seen above, they had their lands confiscated and some were arrested over their fight with a neighboring plantation owner.

The Loangos were also within the orbit of the Catholic Church. In the aftermath of the insurrection, Coro's city council complained about an "abundance of the people of this infamous plebe." They stated that proof of their numbers was found in local baptism records, suggesting that most had undergone the Catholic ceremony.[386] But the ayuntamiento added that the Loangos had not had spiritual support for over a year.

Caracas's Archbishop Mariano Martí anticipated the ayuntamiento's concern 21 years before the insurrection. He reported that Coro's sierra was fully populated and that many were "blacks who came from the island of Curazao."[387] Martí added that because priests were set up in towns surrounding the sierra, and not in the hills themselves, the Loangos had been lacking spiritual attention.

Coro's officials thought that this lack of guidance—coupled with the racist tropes they believed—lent the Loangos to criminal behavior. In the ayuntamiento's 1795 report, they complained that the Loangos' "conduct is corrupt and incorrigible," and that Coro's jails were filled with Loangos, most of whom were imprisoned for stealing from local haciendas.[388] It is indeed possible that some Loangos engaged in the theft of cattle, crops, and tools from neighboring plantations, as this was a common practice among maroon communities in the hemisphere.[389]

---

385 Thompson, 223.
386 "Informe": "abundancia de gente de la infima plebe."
387 Mariano Martí, *Documentos relativos a su visita pastoral de la Diócesis de Caracas (1771-1784): providencias* (Caracas: ANH, 1969), 64: "negros venidos de la isla de Curazao."
388 Ibid.: "conducta es estragada e incorrigible."
389 Thompson, 239.

González himself may have been sought for burglary 15 years before the insurrection. A 1780 investigation by Coro's Justicia Mayor was carried out against Josef Colina, racially classified as pardo, and Josef Charidad Moreno, the last name indicating his black skin color. (During this period in history, the spelling of names was not standardized, so individuals' legal records included various spellings of their names). Colina and Charidad were accused of carrying out various robberies of cattle and crops from the haciendas in Adaure, which neighbored their cumbé. Several witnesses were brought in to testify that they had seen Colina in the act of stealing agricultural goods, but the accused denied any wrongdoing. Josef Charidad was never found or questioned about these accusations, and Colina's fate is not documented.

Because the Josef Charidad pursued in this case was never found, it is impossible to say if he is the same individual accused of masterminding the insurrection. And although Coro's sheriff was carrying out the investigation, Adaure lay 50 miles from the city and 70 miles from the sierra. Whether or not this person was González, the incident does point to the fact that at least one cumbé inhabitant of the region was being sought for stealing hacienda products.[390]

The political economy of the Loango cumbés of Coro was homologous to that of maroon communities throughout the Americas. Although unable to break completely away from colonial control, some maroon collectives enjoyed significant autonomy. The Loangos maintained their native languages and developed new ones. They had their own legal system, yet they sometimes found themselves in trouble with officials. Finally, the Loangos practiced an agrarian lifestyle in which land, its fruits, and its game were available to all members. These

---

[390] "Contra José Colina y José Caridad Moreno por robo," 1780-1781, Casos Criminales, AHF.

practices were not created in a vacuum: They were based upon the social relations of their homelands.

The Gold Coast

Although he may have been born enslaved, the world-renowned abolitionist, Quoba Ottobah Cugoano, lived a carefree childhood. In his 1787 memoir, the Gold Coast native wrote that his upbringing was filled with moments of "peace and tranquility." But like all kids, he and his friends also enjoyed playing games, roughhousing, and breaking rules. They were often "too venturesome" and they would regularly go deep "into the woods to gather fruit and catch birds, and such amusements that pleased" them.[391]

Cugoano was born in the coastal town of Ajumako. His father was "a companion" to the town's chief, so Cugoano grew up in a king-sized residence with his kin as well as other families.[392] As was common for enslaved people in Indigenous communities, Cugoano was sent to live with others throughout his childhood. First with the leader's nephew after the chief passed away, then he stayed with his own uncle who had "hundreds of relations," meaning that he had many wives and children. Although he may have been a slave, Cugoano was seemingly unaware—he was treated as family wherever he lived.[393]

But the young boy's fortunes quickly changed. "Several great ruffians" confronted him and his buddies while they were on a routine jaunt. The villains claimed that the kids "had committed a fault against their lord." As the lads ran away, the bad guys stopped them by pulling out "pistols and cutlasses."[394]

---

391 Quobna Ottobah Cugoano, *Thoughts and Sentiments on the Evil of Slavery* (New York: Penguin Books, 1999), 12.
392 Ibid.
393 Ibid.
394 Ibid., 13.

The youngsters were kidnapped. After traveling a considerable distance, they were placed in separate homes. Desperate to return to his community, Cugoano spent six days in the residence of an unfamiliar man. He refused to eat until the stranger promised that he would take him back to his uncle. Cugoano finally ate "a little fruit with him" but the man had lied. Cugoano would not go home.[395] Soon the child would face ruffians of an even more nefarious nature when he "saw several white people, which made me afraid that they would eat me."[396]

The pale-faced men did not ingest the 13-year-old in the literal sense, but Cugoano's life would be consumed by the Atlantic slave trade. After his abduction, he slaved away in the Caribbean until he attained freedom. Cugoano would then dedicate his life to denouncing the institution and seeking its destruction.

Many of Coro's Loangos were enslaved in the same region and in the identical manner that Cugoano was. And as his contemporaries, some could have encountered the renowned abolitionist at some point in their lives. These origins were not lost in Coro. Royal authorities usually referred to maroons as Loangos, but they did sometimes write "Loango or *mina*" in official records.

Mina was an ethnic marker used in the Atlantic to refer to someone with origins on the Gold Coast. The term mina was taken from Elmina, the name of the largest fort of the region. The name Elmina was a variant of the original designation that the Portuguese gave the castle, São Jorge da Mina—Mina meaning mine. They referred to the region as Costa da Mina because of its large gold deposits.[397]

Social, political and economic customs on Costa da Mina, or the Gold Coast, informed those of maroon

---

395 Ibid., 14.
396 Ibid.
397 Ivor Wilks, *Forests of Gold: Essays on the Akan and the Kingdom of Asante* (Athens: Ohio University Press, 1993), 4.

settlements throughout the Americas. Collective husbandry interfaced with communalist principles to create a rather economically egalitarian society. The heads of households (usually men) were responsible for the home's other members, whose numbers could be in the dozens. This practice expanded to the levels of the town itself, the larger confederation of villages, and the kingdom.[398] This system was aided by the hegemonic conception of consanguinity in which community members were thought of as kin—brothers and sisters—connected by a common ancestor.

The region known as the Gold Coast was roughly coterminous to present-day Ghana. The territory's largest ethnic group was the Akan, who inhabited the forests of the interior of the coast up to the Black Volta River. The Ga was the second biggest ethnicity, and they lived mostly along the eastern coast. The autochthonous peoples of the Gold Coast are known as the Guan. During the 18th century, the Guan lived amongst both the Akan and the Ga, although they were mostly concentrated on the coast, near Winneba. The Ga and the Akan spoke mutually intelligible Kwa languages. Although it is a matter of controversy regarding when the two latecomers arrived at the Gold Coast, it was probably at some point in the 13th century.[399] Greater Asante, the Akan's largest state during the 18th century, was the Gold Coast's most powerful Indigenous group.[400] The Asante rose to authority during the 15th and 16th centuries, when they developed an agrarian society.

---

398 K.Y. Daaku, "Aspects of Precolonial Akan Economy," *The International Journal of African Historical Studies* 5:2 (1972): 245.

399 Kwame Yeboa Daaku, *Trade and Politics on the Gold Coast, 1600-1720* (Oxford: The Clarendon Press, 1970), 1-2; J.K. Flynn, *Asante and Its Neighbors, 1700-1807* (London: Northwestern University Press, 1971), 4.

400 I follow Kwame Arhin's decision to avoid the term "empire" when discussing the Asante, and utilize the term Greater Asante instead. As historians have made clear, Asante expansion had the effect of uniting a people, making this expansionary process quite different than imperialism. See: Kwame Arhin, "The Structure of Greater Ashanti (1700-1824)," *The Journal of African History* 8:1 (1967): 65-85.

Akan polities and those of the Ga and Guan followed a social system whose basis was the home. A typical household comprised a family head, usually a male and a father. Polygamy was common, and the head of the house could have one or more wives. The residence also included unmarried children, married sons and their families, the household head's mother, younger brothers and unmarried sisters, and the sons and daughters of the head of the home's married sisters. Servants were also considered part of the family, so pawns, as well as enslaved people and their descendants, were considered kin.[401]

Agriculture was the basis of economic activity. Men, free and enslaved, cleared forests to cultivate the terrain. This practice was the most labor-intensive aspect of production, but the bulk of it was carried out once every three years. Men would cut down trees, fence fields, and weed them during the clearing period. Families cultivated about two and a half acres of land every three years before the grounds were abandoned for new ones. The soil of the cleared terrain had to be fallowed every three years, and it could not be replanted until the soil recuperated, which took at least ten years.[402]

Women and children harvested the crops, while men raised the livestock.[403] Families planted cereals, fruits and vegetables, such as rice, maize, yam, cassava, and pineapples.[404] Men in the family reared cattle, sheep, goats, pigs, horses, and donkeys.[405] The planting and harvesting of agricultural goods may have required as little as 83 work days every three years. This would have given women and children ample time for arts, educa-

---

401 Akosua Adoma Perbi, *A History of Indigenous Slavery in Ghana: From the 15th to the 19th Century* (Legon: Sub-Saharan Publishers, 2004), 112.
402 Wilks, 46-63.
403 My usage of the terms "women" and "men" is not meant to naturalize these concepts, which are socially constructed. But indigenous Africans and European imperialists used the terms, and these corresponded to the gendered divisions of labor, which existed in the African Atlantic.
404 Wilks, 52; Perbi, 72.
405 Perbi, 75.

tion and leisure, as well as other economic activities, such as handicrafts and marketing.[406] During the 18th century, men used guns, spears, and bows and arrows to hunt for consumption and sale. Search teams left their homes early in the morning and returned in the evening with food and/or ivory.[407] One early 19th-century Tatar traveler noted that Gold Coast hunters dipped their arrows in poison. Sometimes, hunters would follow their prey for days.[408] Fishing was most important on the coast, where men cast their lines and nets, and women prepared the meat.[409]

Independent producers also extracted gold. Women withdrew much of the precious metal by panning in riverbeds, loose alluvium deposits, and coastal sand. This activity was not taxed, and was open to anyone. But local leaders also engaged in gold extrication as an industrial activity, employing enslaved men as miners.[410] Before the slave trade took over the region's economy during the 17th century, gold was the primary commodity traded to foreigners. In fact, Gold Coast peoples had provided the metal to European markets since the ancient Roman period.[411]

Asante groups were considered an enlarged nuclear family, so part of the government's role was to ensure that all had access to an equitable share of their inheritance.[412] In the 18th century, the holder of the Asante Golden Stool was considered head of state. The Queen mother, who held veto power, assisted him in his duties. Senior elders, who were in charge of the army, were next in the hierarchy.[413] The holder of the Stool was the trustee of all land, but in practice, its custodians were

---

406 Wilks, 60.
407 Ibid., 76.
408 Wargee of Astrakhan, "The African Travels of Wargee," in *Africa Remembered: Narratives by West Africans from the Era of the Slave Trade*, ed. Philip D. Curtin (Prospect Heights, Illinois: Waveland Press, 1967), 181.
409 Ibid., 76-7.
410 Ibid., 83-7.
411 Perbi, 83.
412 Daaku, "Aspects," 245.
413 Ibid., 94.

town leaders or chiefs. These sub-chiefs were entrusted with ensuring that all community members could cultivate. Family heads were awarded territory, which was then divided to each member of the household.[414] In a similar vein, marketing and trade were free to all individuals and families, with minimal state interference.

But Asante society was far from idyllic and its government had its fair share of enemies. Before the turn of the century, the Asante began uniting various towns surrounding Kumasi, which became their capital. By 1701, the group had grown so much that they began refusing tribute payments to the Denkyira, which was the strongest kingdom of the period. Although the Asante were able to establish themselves as the ruling government of the Gold Coast, Denkyira loyalists were still dispersed throughout the region, and they refused to pledge allegiance.[415] Other towns rejected the amount of tribute that they were responsible for paying, and still others refused the presence of the Asante military.[416] The country thus found itself in a continuous flow of conflict, which fed the Atlantic slave trade.

Most people on the Gold Coast were enslaved by way of warfare, whether they remained in the region or were traded to Europeans. Contemporary oral histories show that 31% of respondents found that warfare was "very important" to acquiring slaves, while 26% noted the importance of local markets. Kidnapping, tribute, and pawning each received 10% of responses.[417]

There were at least 63 indigenous slave markets in the Gold Coast. Thirty of them were seaside, and the remaining 33 were scattered across the interior.[418] At these markets, enslaved individuals were traded for an assortment of other commodities, such as cowry shells,

---

414 Daaku, *Trade*, 50-1; Daaku, "Aspects," 241-5.
415 Daaku, *Trade*, 144-60.
416 Ibid., 78.
417 Perbi, 28.
418 Ibid., 37.

ivory, iron, weapons, and textiles. European goods were highly regarded and always available.

Salaga was the region's largest market. It lay 120 miles northeast of Kumasi, and 240 miles from the coastline. Buyers and sellers from as far as present-day Burkina Faso and Nigeria would go there to trade. Salaga's market was divided into two sections: one for dealing slaves and the second for selling other goods. Merchandise was placed on top of mats that lay on the ground. Enslaved people were chained in groups of 10 to 15, united by fetters across their necks and waists.[419] Many of these individuals never made it to European ships, and lived their lives as slaves on the Gold Coast.

Slavery in the region was radically different than in the Americas. Although enslaved people were marked by their condition, they still held many of the same rights as other family members. They had the same freedom to plant, eat, trade, to be clothed, and to receive protection. Enslaved people on the Gold Coast could have independent incomes, could own property, and they could inherit their master's possessions. Slaves could also rise to positions of authority. In fact, 20% of Asante stools, or royal office appointments, were held by enslaved people.[420]

But slavery did limit one's possibilities in life, and enslaved people were ultimately considered a separate, lower class. Enslaved men and women ate with the free women of the home, separated from the free men. They were also expected to dress modestly and were barred from wearing gold. The status of enslaved people was not forgotten during their lifetimes. It was not until the third or fourth generation that they could be considered equal members of their families.[421]

Gold Coast society molded life in the Loango cumbés. A political economy rooted in communal agriculture, and buttressed by independent industry, hunting, gathering,

---

419 Ibid., 47.
420 Ibid., 142.
421 Ibid., 113-32.

Map of the Gold Coast.

and trade, was practiced in the West African region and in Coro's settlements. Despite significant divisions—of class, ethnicity, politics, and sex—notions of consanguinity and an equitable distribution of resources united Gold Coast communities. The Loango Coast was no different.

The Loango Coast

As the world's largest human depot for the Atlantic slave trade, as well as the home of a mystical, once dominant kingdom, the Loango Coast cast a spell on Europe's literary élite. Nowhere was this truer than in France, whose formidable Empire operated on the blood, sweat and tears of African people, many hailing from the notorious coastline. Several French travelers visited the Loango region during the early modern period and published chronicles of their adventures when they returned home.

Perhaps the most notable title was Liévain Bonaventure Proyart's 1776 book *Histoire de Loango, Kakongo, et autres Royaumes d'Afrique*. Proyart dedicated nearly half of his 400-pages proto-ethnographical work to the study of societal customs on the coast—religious practices, as well as marriage ceremonies, family relations, language, commerce, and government. He described the peoples of the region as "human and obliging, even toward strangers, and those from whom they expect nothing in return."[422] They were "willing to share the little they have with those they know to be in need." Finally, he added, "if they be happy in hunting or fishing, and have obtained some rare piece, they also run to give notice to their friends and neighbors, carrying them their share."[423]

Typical of travelers' accounts during the period, Proyart painted a picture of a benevolent yet backward people. Given the text's proximity to the French Revolution and major tracts on the equality of man, one could think that this was the fantastical representation of a utopian projecting his ideals onto a foreign society. But if this were the case, Proyart did not fit the bill. He was a devout Catholic and a loyal servant to Louis XVI. He was a staunch and notable opponent of the French Revolution, the author of a scathing biography on Maximilien Robespierre called *Vie et crimes de Robespierre, surnommé le tyran* (Life and Crimes of Robespierre, Known as The Tyrant). Although patronizing and fanciful, Proyart's account of the Loango Coast provides rare first-hand details that cannot be found elsewhere.

In the 18th century, the Loango Coast was home to three ethnic groups, which had their respective kings and ports of trades. The Vili of the Kingdom of Loango were the dominant polity for much of the early modern period

---

422 L'Abbé Proyart, *Histoire de Loango, Kakongo, et autres Royaumes d'Afrique* (Paris, 1776), 71: "ils sont prêts à partager le peu qu'ils ont avec qu'ils savent être dans le besoin."

423 Ibid.: "s'ils ont été heureux à la chasse ou à la pêche, & qu'ils se foient procure quelque piece rare, ils courent aussi-tôto en donner avis à leurs amis & à leurs voisins, en leur en portant leur part."

until the Ngoyo and Kakongo Kingdoms achieved independence during the mid-18th century. The Loango realm was 120 miles long and stretched from the ChiLoango River to the Banya lagoon. It had four provinces, of which Loangiri (also known as Loango) was home to the capital of Buali, and was the main trading point of the Loango Bay. The people of the Kingdom of Ngoyo identified as the Woyo, and they held the port of Cabinda. The smallest of the three realms, the Kakongo, was of the Kotchi people who held their port at Malemba. All three polities had similar cultural and institutional practices and they spoke mutually intelligible dialects of Kikongo, a Bantu language.[424]

Homes on the Loango Coast consisted of 10 to 40 people who practiced collective agriculture.[425] Women in the family planted and harvested the fields with items like beans, cassava, yams, and maize.[426] Free men, and probably enslaved ones too, cleared a new field out of the forest once a year. They then built a fence around the grounds and planted traps to keep animals out. Yams were an important staple in a family's diet. Women harvested the vegetables 10 months after planting them. Men would then help stack them. Land was then left to fallow. Small greens would grow during this period, however, and they were added to the family's selection of foods. A small portion of the terrain was kept to grow kitchen crops until a new field was planted.

Homes needed 10 times the amount of land they cultivated to maintain themselves. This meant that fresh fields would lie farther away from the town as time passed. About once every ten years, a village would migrate to new lands once the distance became too great.[427]

---

[424] Phyllis M. Martin, *The External Trade of the Loango Coast, 1576-1870: The Effects of Changing Commercial Relations on the Vili Kingdom of Loango* (Oxford: The Clarendon Press, 1972), 3-30.

[425] Jan Vasina, *Paths in the Rainforests, Towards a History of Political Tradition in Equatorial Africa* (London: James Currey, 1990), 75.

[426] Martin, 13; Vasina, 84-5.

[427] Vasina, 85-99.

But farming was meant to produce only 40% of the home's food supply. Animal traps steadily supplied meat. Families also hunted, fished, gathered fruits and vegetables, and grew colonies of edible insects. Households also made pottery, cloth, and baskets, which were bartered for foodstuff.[428]

As was the case in the Gold Coast, Loango Coast societies were imagined as an expanded version of the home. Three interlocking zones formed the basis of society: the district, the village, and the house. The house was led by a polygamous man who acted as father to a host of kin and servants, as well as friends. Marriages occurred in many ways: Sisters could be exchanged amongst male heads of families, women could be married off as a form of payment, or given away as a gift. Women were also wed through violent force—when they were granted as compensation from the losing party in a war or, in rare cases, if they were abducted.[429]

The structure of a village followed a similar logic to that of the home. Each town had a leader who had earned, rather than inherited, his title. Towns had around 100 inhabitants who shared three to ten rectangular homes that lay along the sides of a road or a plaza. Each town also had a communal shed, which was shared by all residents for activities like weaving, carpentry, and smithing.[430]

Each village had a central area designated for community meetings, including those of the town's leader and his council. Here, plans were collectively made and disputes were handled. The town's head commanded respect from all residents. He and his home were always provided the largest share of a hunt, and he was invariably awarded the most emblematic animals killed, such as the leopard.[431]

---

428 Ibid., 83-5.
429 Vasina, 75-7.
430 Ibid.
431 Ibid., 77-9.

Finally, the district was a loosely organized confederation of towns that subscribed to a common identity. The district did not have a leader entrusted with its care. Rather, neighboring chiefs communicated with each other to address issues of mutual interest. When entire towns migrated every ten years to work new fields, they tended to stay within the vicinity of their district, which had the effect of creating and maintaining a group identity.[432]

The Kingdom of Loango united the districts of the coast for much of the 18th century. Before the Ngoyo and Kakongo Kingdoms gained independence, they were tied to the Kingdom of Loango as junior partners who paid tribute.[433] But even after they split from the Loango Crown, they continued to pay some taxes.[434]

The King of Loango, known as the Maloango, held his throne at the city of Buali, just a few miles in from the coast. Unlike the leaders of the towns, as well as the King of Asante, the Loango king's title was hereditary. Yet Proyart notes that the Maloango's wealth was not radically superior to that of commoners. The Frenchman attested that his palace consisted of only "five or six houses, a little larger" than those of average families.[435]

All towns and homes paid tribute to the King, but the amount was proportional to their means. Homes with fewer occupants and less land paid a lower rate than those that had more. Tribute payments were made in both labor and kind, and were collected by royal officials during their regular visits.

By the mid-18th century, the Loango Kingdom witnessed the rise of merchants who gained influence through their participation in the slave trade. Although prominent, the merchants, known as Mafouks, were not rich. Proyart wrote, "the bourgeois have nothing that

---

432 Ibid., 81-2.
433 Martin, 22.
434 Christina Frances Mobley, "The Kongolese Atlantic: Central African Slavery & Culture from Mayombe to Haiti" (Ph.D. diss.: Duke University, 2015), 70.
435 Proyart, 57: "cinq ou six cases, un peu plus grandes."

distinguishes them from the villagers; they are neither better dressed nor better housed. The bourgeoisie of the capital will work in the fields, like the peasant women of the smallest hamlet."[436]

Despite their lack of wealth, the emergence of the Mafouks eroded the power of the Maloango, contributed to a political breakdown in the region, and led to war. After the Kakongo and Ngoyo Crowns gained independence from the Moloango, they began receiving threats from inland groups. Polities from the interior were eager to become direct providers of enslaved people to Europeans by getting rid of Ngoyo and Kakongo middlemen. Disputes over legitimacy in the two breakaway Loango states also contributed to an outbreak of civil wars, which coincided with the slave trade's peak between 1763 and 1793. Mafouks, who mostly lived on or near the coast, also began fighting over territory.[437]

It is important to note, however, that warfare on the Loango Coast was not as destructive as it was in Europe and its colonies. There were two types of wars waged during the proto-colonial period: restricted wars and destructive wars. Restricted wars, by far the most common form of warfare, were fought in accordance with strict rules. The leaders of the two communities in conflict would meet to agree upon a day in which battle would be waged. The two parties would then come face to face on the borders of the two fighting districts. After one or two men were seriously injured or killed, peace negotiations would commence and compensation was negotiated.

Destructive wars were extremely rare. The term "destructive war" comes from the Bantu word "to burn" because the communities of the losing party were burned to the ground. These campaigns were designed to destroy or chase away an enemy, take their lands,

---

436 Ibid., 54-5.: "Les bourgeois n'ont rien quiles distingue des villageois: ils ne sont ni mieux vêtus, ni mieux loges. Les bourgeoises de la capitale vont travailler aux champs, comme les paysannes du plus petit hameau."
437 Mobley, 64-107.

and subordinate those who were defeated.[438] When seen within this context, the Coro rebellion had all the markings of a destructive war.

But the result of all conflicts, whether restricted or destructive, was enslavement. The losing party would transfer ownership of enslaved people to the winning side, and some free community members would be converted to slaves and handed to the victorious faction. Many of these individuals would then be sold to Europeans.

People were enslaved not only through war, but also through kidnapping, inheritance and, perhaps most significantly, criminal prosecution. Penalties for crimes, such as fighting, failure to pay debt, and witchcraft grew throughout the 18th century because of the stimulus provided by the slave trade. The punishment for these crimes increasingly became enslavement.[439]

But many enslaved people lived out their lives in Loango, as part of an institution similar to the one that operated on the Gold Coast. Writing of his travels in 1786, Frenchman Louis de Grandpré stated, "many (servants) are slaves and subject to the caprices of their master, who sells them according to his will."[440] But the visitor stressed that the practice was different from what it was in the Americas. He wrote, "though law places them there as slaves; either that their wealth gives them a consideration that shelters them, or that a long filiation in the place of their residency has made them so natural that their master is afraid to sell them."[441] De Grandpré observed that while enslaved people were considered a

---

438 Vasina, 80.
439 Ibid., 159.
440 L. de Grandpré, *Voyage à la côte occidentale d'Afrique, fait dans les années 1786 et 1787* (Paris, 1801), 105: "sont esclaves et soumis aux caprices de leur maître, qui les vend suivant sa volonté."
441 Ibid.: "quoique la loi les y assujettisse comme esclaves; mais soit que leur richesse leur donne une consideration qui les met à l'abri, soit qu'une longue filiation dans le lieu de leur residence, les y ait tellement naturalizes que leur maître craigne de les vendre."

class below ordinary citizens and could be sold off at a whim, they also had the right to assert themselves, as well as acquire property and power. Although violent conflict was prevalent during certain periods, and divisions of class, ethnicity and sex were a permanent feature of life, Loango Coast communities operated on the basis that all group members were entitled to a fair share of resources. Kings, chiefs and merchants were not radically wealthier than commoners or even enslaved individuals. Political and economic practices were conducted in such a way as to ensure that all people had access to food, shelter, and clothing. These customs are seen in the Loango cumbés, and are at least partially responsible for the egalitarian notions that Coro's insurgents espoused.

Conclusion

Soon after González and his two anonymous comrades were murdered, nine other Loangos suffered the same fate. On the night of May 14, their wives tried to bribe a jailer to let their husbands escape. But their plan was swiftly thwarted and the women were imprisoned. The following day, Ramírez Valderraín decapitated the nine Loangos.[442]

On May 23, the soon to be disgraced sheriff continued his brutal acts of retribution. He sentenced 53 people, including 22 Loangos, to terrible destinies, distinguished only by their degree of dreadfulness. He ruled that 21 legally free and enslaved Black men were to have their throats slit. Three enslaved women—Polonia, Juana Antonia, and Trinidad—were to receive 200 lashes each and be sold outside of Coro if they survived their punishment. Seven Indigenous men were sentenced to 10 years of hard labor in Puerto Cabello. The 22 Loangos were ordered to join the native American prisoners for six years, "to serve your Majesty for rations and without

---

442 "Expediente," ff. 9.

wages."[443] It remains unknown whether or not these freshly enslaved people survived their new toils.

Soon after these sentences were meted out, Comandante Francisco Jacot ordered that more Loangos be rounded up and sent to Puerto Cabello. On June 7, the Captain stated, "I conferenced with the Justicia Mayor about whether it would be convenient to expatriate the black Luangos, or minas."[444] Five days later, Jacot expounded on his position to the Captain General, stating that there were 250 Black and pardo free people living in the sierra. These individuals were "added to the haciendas without a home, nor property, corrupting the servants with their depraved customs and most of them took part in the rebellion in order to rob, or as compliant troops, but it is difficult to prove for many."[445]

Jacot added that the Loangos in the sierra should be taken to Puerto Cabello because if "they are not totally expatriated this land will not be secure."[446] A few weeks later, Jacot and Ramírez Valderraín partly got their wish. Not all of the Loangos were rounded up, but 42 adult men and 10 of their underage sons were taken from their homes and sent to labor camps.[447]

But Puerto Cabello's authorities rejected the imposition. When the city's Captain, Antonio Guillelmi, reported that the Loangos had arrived, he complained, "there is no room to receive more prisoners without grave danger for their security because we no longer have bodegas, jails, nor other locations where they can be secured."[448]

---

443 Ibid., ff. 1-3: "varias veces las armas que se le denegaron"; "a que sirvan a su Magestad a racion y sin sueldo."

444 Ibid., ff. 51-2: "conferencie con el Justicia Mayor sobre si coviene expatriar los negros Luangos, o minas."

445 Ibid., ff. 53-4: "agregados a las haciendas sin domicilio, ni propiedad, corrompiendo a los criados con sus depravadas constumbres y los mas de ellos concurrieron a la rebellion asi para rrobar, o como efectivos complices dificl de probarselo a muchos."

446 Ibid.: "no se expatrien totalmente no quedara aseguarada esta tierra."

447 Ibid.: ff. 147: "viejos inutiles."

448 Ibid., ff. 256: "no hay ya donde recivir mas presos sin gravissimo peligro de su seguridad por no tenerse ya mas bodegas, carceles, ni otros parajes donde aseguralos."

Guillelmi suggested that if Coro's authorities were to send any more captives, they should be sent to Caracas because Puerto Cabello simply could not feed or house any more inmates.

The Court—the *Real Audiencia de Caracas*—was tasked with coming up with a solution to this crisis. On September 28, they ruled that because the Loangos could no longer be held in Puerto Cabello, they should be sent to fight for Spain in its war against revolutionary France. So the prisoners were dispatched to the "Ships of the Flotilla for as long as the War lasts."[449]

But over a year later, the Audiencia made a stunning about-face. On December 10, 1796, they declared, "the black Luangos entirely free of involvement in the expressed uprising, and that they are loyal servants of the King and of the public, commanding that they be returned to the care of their homes, and families."[450] The court added that whether they were in Caracas, Puerto Cabello, or fighting for the King overseas, all Loangos should be taken back to Coro. After having spent a year and a half in prison and/or fighting the war in Saint-Domingue, the Loangos were shockingly declared innocent.

The Audiencia's declaration raises just as many questions as it provides answers. González and the other Loangos killed were not mentioned in the court's ruling. Therefore, it is unclear whether or not they were also pronounced innocent. Perhaps feeling secure that victory in Coro was assured, the tribunal could have determined that the Loangos were no longer a threat. They may have succumbed to pressure from the prisoners' families and extended networks to return them home. Or maybe the court came across indisputable evidence that vindicated the Loangos. If the latter scenario were true, however, the Audiencia did not provide details.

---

449 "Expedientes, sublevación de esclavos," ff. 56-7: "Baxeles de la Esquadra por el tiempo que dure la Guerra."

450 "Expediente," ff. 6.: "entteramentte libres de complicidad en la expresada subleacion a los negros Luangos, y que son fieles servidores del Rey y del publico, mandando que sean restituidos al cuidado de sus casas, y familias."

Although the full story may never be known, it is clear that at least a handful of Loangos participated in the 1795 insurrection. And it is easy to see why. Although legally free, the Loangos were forced to fight for their land and faced severe penalties for their struggle. Like the rest of Coro's "free" people, the Loangos were also targets of excessive taxes and lived at the mercy of capricious authorities.

Hardships such as these encouraged Coro's revolutionaries to take up arms and establish a society free of degrading inequalities. The equitable political and economic systems of autochthonous towns in West and West Central Africa provided a model for a new republic, as it did for maroon settlements across the Americas, including the Loango cumbés.

Communal production in Gold and Loango Coast towns ensured material parity within these societies. Under this system, subsistence was secure, and output was restricted. This prevented a large surplus from being produced, one that could be usurped by high-ranking members of the population. Although external markets did distort this political economy, they were unable to refashion its essence. When combined with the egalitarian trends of the Atlantic, as well as the harsh conditions under which the rebels lived, this experience with concrete equality was a powder keg that could explode on Coro's plantation system at any moment.

But the region's Black people were not the only ones who imagined a more just political and economic order. Coro's Indigenous rebels were also buoyed by dreams of a communalist society that would be built upon the ashes of colonial rule.

Chapter 4

Indigenous Labor-Power

While atrocities were being carried out in the city center of Coro, José Leonardo Chirino and the sierra's insurgents were planning revenge. They settled on the Macanillas plantation and were using it to plan and launch attacks. The rebels reacted to their defeats by requesting support from Pecaya, an Ajagua town that lay 15 miles southeast.

Chirino himself wrote a message to the town's Native authorities:

> Sir Casique, and Sir Captain, and Sir Governor, my dear sirs, finding myself in this effort to see if these burdens which kill us will end, requesting the people that you are able to give me, so that I can go make a good entrance to Coro, to see if we seize them, so that we may have some relief; with this, you will not pay for a delay, and this is what is offered for now; I beg to God that he keep me many years. From your affectionate servant that kisses your hands, Josef Leonardo Chirino.[451]

Born to an Indigenous mother in the Ajagua town of Pedregal, Chirino sought support from their officials—Governor

---

[451] "Expedientes, sublevacion de esclavos," ff. 337: "Señor Casique, y el Señor Capitan, y el Señor Governador, mui señores mios hallándome en este empeño de ver si se acaban estos pechos que nos matan, proponiendo a Vds la gente que me pueden dar, para ir a hacer le una dentrada buena a Coro, a ver si lo cojemos, para tener algun alivio, con eso, no pagaran demora, y es quanto se ofrece por ahora, rogar a Dios me guarde muchos años=De su afectísimo servidor que besa sus manos, Josef Leonardo Chirino."

153

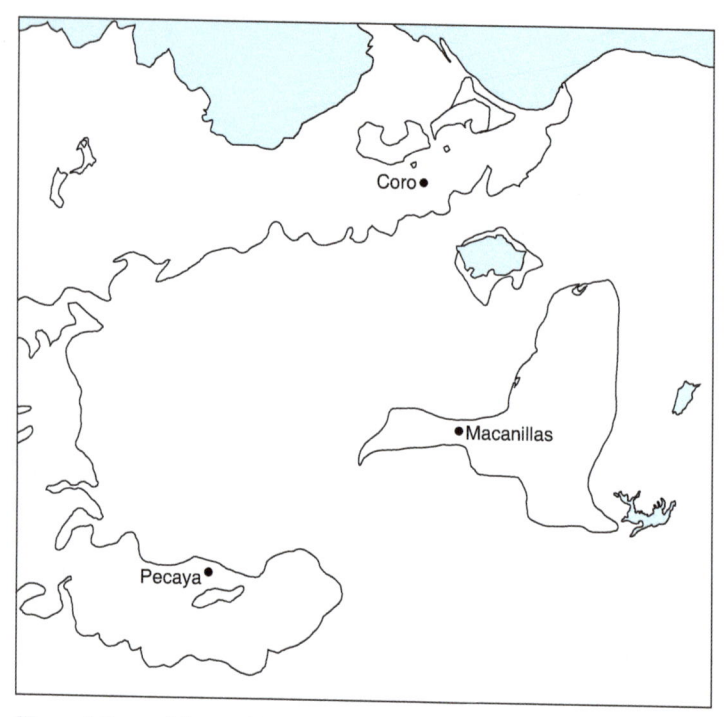

Map of Coro, Macanillas and Pecaya.

Don Joseph Bernandino Carencio, Cacique Don Balthasar Carencio and Captain Don Juan Ygnocencio Tua.[452] After the note was drawn up, a Caquetío rebel named Juan de Mata was charged with delivering the missive.

Chirino recognized that the rebels had common cause with the Ajagua. He realized that they too wanted the "burden" of taxes removed. Coro's Indigenous peoples rejected these impositions. Despite having endured hundreds of years of European rule, Native peasants continued to pursue economic activities that clashed with Coro's tax system, not to mention the very nature of colonialism.

But at the time of the insurrection, a dramatic increase in alcabala exaction pushed Indigenous people further away from the lifestyles they esteemed.

---

452 Ibid., ff. 387.

This cut into their ability to sustain themselves, and forced them to supplement autochthonous labor practices with wage work on haciendas and plantations. This burden was made worse by the other taxes that Indigenous people were already forced to pay: tribute, Church contributions, and *corregidor* fees, which supported the colonial office dedicated to policing Indigenous communities.

As to Chirino's letter, it looks like Ajagua's leaders never received it. Months after the insurrection, Pecaya's governor denied getting it, adding that he never met Chirino, nor had ever heard of him. Pecaya's corregidor, Don Hilario Bustos, supported the governor's statement when he relayed his story of being kidnapped by "blacks."[453] Bustos stated, "because it was a work day I always leave the Indians and neighbors defenseless because they are attending to their crops and labors. I found myself suddenly attacked by more than thirty blacks who apprehended me, armed with shotguns, lances, machetes, and axes."[454] As corregidor, Bustos was in charge of ensuring that Indigenous people paid their taxes and were busy working. His account was meant to indicate that the Natives under his watch, including those of Pecaya, were not involved in the insurrection.

But Bustos's contention was inaccurate. Although Indigenous communities did not participate in the rebellion in an official manner, native American individuals were deeply involved from the start. After all, the revolutionary leader himself was Indigenous. When the first blows were struck on the night of May 10, two of the four men that were by Chirino's side were Native. These men—Juan de los Santos, a Caquetío from Carrizal and

---

453 "Expediente sobre la insurrección de los negros, zambos y mulatos proyectada en el año 1795 a las inmediaciones de la ciudad de Coro, Provincia de Caracas," 1795, Caracas, 426, AGI, ff. 241-44.

454 Ibid.: "por ser dia de trabajo siempre está desamparado de los yndios, y vecinos que estan attendiendo a sus cosechas, y lavores, me vi acometido repentinamentte de mas de treintta negros armados de escopetas, lansas, machettes, y tacises, que me prendieron."

Pedro Coyo, an Ajagua—helped their accomplices kill Don Josef de Martínez.[455]

People of Indigenous descent continued their participation in the hours that followed. Like Chirino, the free zambos Candelario and Juan Christóval were residents at the Socorro plantation and among the first to take up arms. Juan de Matos, the Caquetío rebel tasked with taking Chirino's message to Pecaya, was a resident of Macanillas and he was by the leader's side during the first days of the insurrection.[456] As mentioned in the first chapter, it appears that the Ajagua man, Juan de Jesús de Lugo, also participated in the uprising even though he claimed to be innocent. Not all rebels were named alongside their racial classification in surviving documents, however. So it is impossible to know exactly how many Indigenous people were involved. Despite this, it is clear that many were.[457]

But native American people played just as decisive a role as soldiers defending the Crown. These efforts began on May 11, when word of the rebellion reached Coro, and several Indigenous people were organized into contingents at the home of Justicia Mayor Ramírez Valderraín. Later that day, two Caquetíos from Carrizal—Cipriano Antonio Gonzales and Lorenzo Reyes Díaz—were injured in the battle at Caujarao, and would later die from their wounds.[458] During the decisive battle on the morning of May 12, 84 Caquetío men comprised nearly 40% of the soldiers that defeated the rebels' largest advance.[459] Being outmanned, colonial forces relied on the Caquetío, their bows and arrows, and their expertise, to crush the rebellion.

The Caquetío, who made up 90% of Coro's Indigenous population, defended the Crown because it was their job

---

455 Ibid., ff. 96-7.
456 Ibid., ff. 92-5.
457 Ibid., ff. 97-102.
458 Ibid., ff. 343.
459 Ibid., ff. 176-7; ff. 350-2.

to do so. The people had been loyal to the metropole since the conquest and they were rewarded with "freedom": the exemption from slavery, the *encomienda*—annual peonage service—and Indigenous tribute payments. But these supposed liberties were traded for contemporary loyalties too, including mandatory military service. This arrangement paid off handsomely for colonial officials, especially during the 1795 insurrection.

Although the Caquetío were tribute-exempt, the Ajaguas and Ayamanes were not. One would assume that these communities sided with the insurgents, but this was not necessarily the case. On the morning of May 15, Ramírez Valderraín sent two expeditions of 100 men each to the sierra to capture any rebels still in arms. Don Juan Ramos de Chaves led one of the two expeditions, which included 104 men. Eighty-four of these soldiers were Ajaguas from Pecaya, Pedregal, and San Luis.[460] The other contingent included a number of Caquetío, although it is unclear how many. These expeditions resulted in the capture of 35 suspected rebels who were executed three days later.[461] The 84 Ajaguas who fought were promised exemption from tribute payments in exchange for their efforts.

Indigenous participation in the 1795 insurrection, as well as its undoing, was the product of a racialized labor system in which native American people played an integral role. A dramatic increase in alcabala collection incensed the region's legally free people, including Natives. These burdens prevented Indigenous peasants from providing themselves adequate food, clothing and shelter, and forced them away from the equitable social practices they valued. This escalation of oppression led some Indigenous people to launch a revolutionary movement and others to seek relief through aiding the Crown. This chapter tells the history of Indigenous labor in Coro,

---

460 Ibid., ff. 9-11; ff. 76.
461 Ibid., ff. 9.

its importance to the functioning of colonial society, and its role in the anti-slavery revolution.

Indigenous Labor until 1721

Legend has it that at the time of the conquest, the Caquetío cacique known as Manaure met with the conquistador Juan Martínez de Ampíes. According to this tale, the celebrated commanders agreed to a deal that would benefit them both. Ampíes would stop Europeans from enslaving the Caquetío and would direct them to kidnap their rivals instead. In exchange, Manaure agreed to let the soon-to-be first governor of Venezuela establish the city of Coro.[462] Some say that the meeting never happened, but hardly anyone refutes that a deal was reached.[463]

Ampíes was not the first European to try to dominate the people and land of *"Tierra Firme,"* the coastal tier of northern South America that would later become known as Venezuela. The earliest attempt came in 1498 under the command of Christopher Columbus. He explored the eastern region of contemporary Venezuela to enslave Indigenous people and sell them in Spain. The following year, another conquistador, Alonso de Ojeda, was the first to inspect the future site of Coro in order to enslave its Natives.[464] Two years later, Ojeda returned to the place that the locals called Todariquiba with a license from Queen Isabel. This permit gave him Spanish authority to establish a new colony. But Caquetío soldiers conquered the conqueror, and they expelled him from the region.

Similar ventures continued until the tide turned in 1511. That year, Queen Isabel declared war against the "Caribs"—any Indigenous people who resisted colonization.

---

462 Ibid., 93-6.
463 "Cacique Manaure" in Biografías Egly Colina Marín Primera. Eglycolinamarinprimera.blogspot.com/2014/11/cacique-manaure-2.html?m=1.
464 Ibid.

Soon after, 2,000 Caquetíos from Todariquiba were enslaved and sent to toil in Santo Domingo.[465] This last event led to Ampíes's conquest of Coro. Some of the Caquetío who were enslaved wound up working on the budding conquistador's property in Hispaniola. Ampíes was impressed with his human cattle, their alleged dedication to Christianity, and their supposedly high work ethic.[466] In 1520, Ampíes sought and received royal permission to establish a settlement on the island of Curaçao. Ampíes took his Caquetío slaves with him and used some of them to establish relations with Cacique Manaure.

The deal with Manaure was a land grab that would strip the region's peoples of their sovereignty and condition the Coro that burned in 1795. During the precolonial period, Indigenous societies were structured similarly to those of the Gold and Loango Coasts. Homes were organized along a sexual and generational division of labor in which resources were sought collectively and shared equitably. This theory and practice carried over to the level of the town and society.

At the time of the conquest, there were four Indigenous peoples that inhabited the region: the Caquetío, the Jirajaras, the Ajaguas, and the Ayamanes. The Caquetíos were the largest and longest established of the four groups, but not much is known about them. They were an Arawak-speaking people who arrived in Coro between 10,000 and 12,000 years ago.[467] At the time of the conquest, the Caquetío inhabited the coastal region of much of the future province of Venezuela, including Coro, and also reached inland toward contemporary Barquisimeto. The Caquetío also lived on the islands that

---

465 Adrián Hernández Baño, *Los Caquetíos de Falcón: Modos de vida* (Coro, Venezuela: Instituto de Cultura del Estado Falcón, 1984), 45. During this period, all native American peoples of the greater Caribbean region were known as "Caribs" if they were hostile to the Crown or considered "uncivilized."
466 Otilia Margarita Rosas González, "La población indígena en la Provincia de Venezuela" (Ph.D. diss.: Universidad de Salamanca, 2015), 91.
467 Jossy M. Mansur, *E indiannan Caquetío* (Aruba: Imprenta Nacional Arubano, 1981), 29.

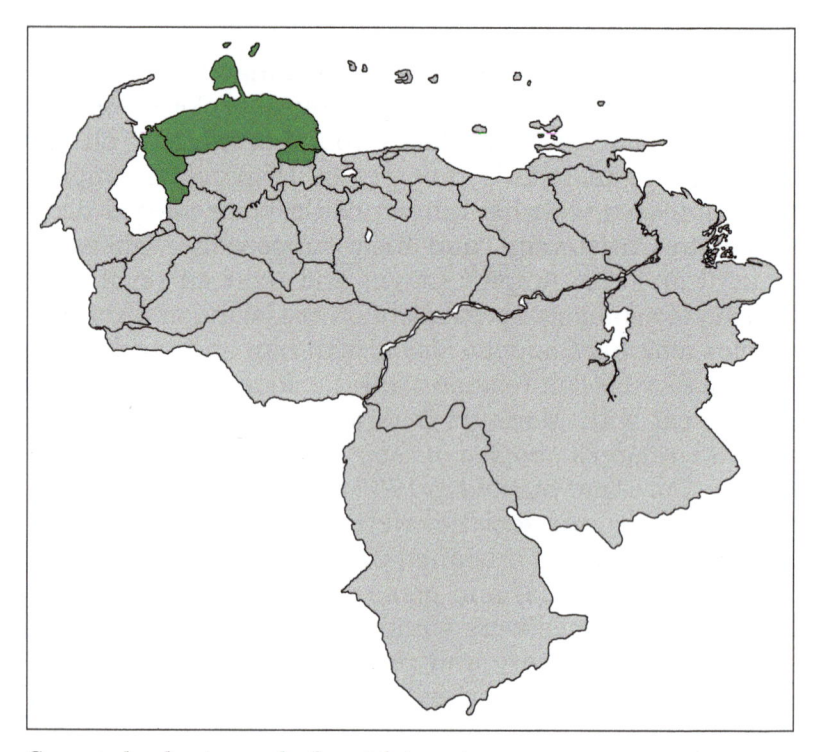

Caqueto land prior to the Spanish invasion.

would become known as Aruba, Bonaire, and Curaçao. These settlements maintained close connections with the mainland before and after the conquest. At the time of the 1795 rebellion, there were 7,000 Caquetío in Coro and they equaled 26% of the population.

Before the conquest, the Caquetío had a sedentary agricultural society in which a cacique was in charge, but where power was dispersed to towns and households. Villages were structured upon the ideal of the family, and all community members were considered descendants of the same ancestor. The patterns of homes differed from town to town but they did share certain characteristics. Houses typically sheltered five or six nuclear families that were all closely related to one another. A town's land was held in common and homes were placed at a distance from one another, erected in

Little is known about the precolonial Caquetío, but even less is known about the Jirajaras, Ajaguas, and Ayamanes. According to the conquistadors, the Jirajaras were the second-largest group of the region at the time of the conquest. They lived in the sierra and south of it. The Jirajaras and the Ayamanes spoke Jirajara, a language that was unique to these two groups.[474] The Ajaguas occupied the mountainous zones west of the sierra, in the settlements that would be named San Luis, Pecaya, and Pedregal. Like the Caquetío, the Ajaguas were Arawak speakers.[475] All of these groups were known hunters and gatherers, although it is likely that they also engaged in agriculture. It is unknown if they paid tribute to Caquetío leaders, but it is important to note that the Jirajaras were the dominant group's enemies at the time of the conquest.[476]

Ampíes would ultimately lose the city of Coro to European rivals, but the relatively privileged position of the Caquetíos would continue throughout the colonial period. Ampíes's plans were ruined the year after he founded Coro when the Spanish Crown gave the German banking family, the Welsners, exclusive rights over Tierra Firme.[477] The Welsners eroded Ampíes's agreements with the Caquetío. But once the Spanish Crown reestablished its domain over Venezuela in 1539, the Province's Bishop Rodrigo Bastidas, declared that the Caquetíos were "*amigos*," "*buena gente*," friendly, good people and loyal vassals of the Spanish Crown.[478]

With this ruling, Bastidas declared the Caquetío exempt from encomienda service, but the rest of the Indigenous population was not.[479] Little is known about the encomienda in Coro, but elsewhere in Venezuela it

---

474 Adelaar, 129.
475 Pedro Manuel Arcaya, *Historia del estado Falcón* (Caracas: Tip. La Nación, 1953), 74.
476 Rosas González, 55-61.
477 Ibid., 97.
478 Ibid., 134.
479 Ibid., 134, 181.

the middle of fields. Polygamy was practiced, but it was likely reserved for important members of each region.[468] The home's "father" assigned tasks to "junior" household members. Men cleared and prepared fields, while women planted and harvested crops such as corn, potatoes, yucca, pineapple and tobacco. Men fished and hunted, while women and children gathered fruit. Men manufactured axes, knives, lances, and bows and arrows, while women created the hammocks on which people slept and the ceramics from which they ate.[469]

Each town practiced some economic activities together while others were carried out on the household level. Because fields were shared, agriculture was conducted cooperatively between neighbors. Hunting and fishing were done in groups of men from various households. Fishing was particularly important for communities near the coast. Hunting for armadillos, deer, elk and rabbits was also done collectively amongst groups of men. Each household provided their own fruits and vegetables that were collected from the wild.[470]

Towns and homes were largely self-sufficient but individuals also traded and paid tribute to the cacique. Salt, tobacco, gold, corn, hammocks, salted fish, and smoked meat were all exchanged at local markets.[471] Town leaders, who earned their titles through merit, were responsible for collecting regular tribute from the townspeople and transporting it to Manaure.[472] The cacique was considered divine and was revered in this way. Early 16th-century European chroniclers wrote that Manaure's followers carried him on their shoulders when he was being transported, so that his feet would not touch the ground.[473]

---

468 Mario Sanoja and Iraida Vargas, *Antiguas formaciones y modos de producción venezolanos* (Caracas: Monte Ávila Editores, 1974), 149-75.
469 Hernández Baño, 26-35.
470 Ibid.
471 Ibid.
472 Ibid., 44; Sanoja and Vargas, 176.
473 Sanoja and Vargas, 175.

was practiced on a rotational basis. Indigenous laborers were required to work for an *encomendero* for one month without pay before they were allowed to return home for two months.[480] The encomienda was abolished in 1721, and thereafter, Coro's Jirajara, Ajagua, and Ayaman peoples were required to pay tribute.

The Spanish invasion of Todariquiba terrorized the Indigenous peoples of the region and transformed autochthonous political and economic systems. The communitarian principles and practices that guided Indigenous towns were replaced by slavery, the encomienda, and colonial rule. These latter arrangements would determine the organization of Indigenous labor in the 18th century, and shape the outcome of the 1795 insurrection. But despite the impositions, Coro's Natives continued executing their communal credos—at least until they couldn't.

Indigenous Labor from 1721 to 1795

On April 14, 1788, the treasurer of Puerto Cabello wrote a frantic letter regarding Indigenous tribute to Venezuela's governor. Miguel de Basterra begged the Captain General to tell Coro to stop sending him their *cocuiza*—cactus-like plants that served as tribute payments. For years, Coro's treasurers had been shipping cocuiza and hammocks to the seaport, where they were auctioned to the public. Cocuiza was the raw material used to produce hammocks, rope and, of particular importance in Puerto Cabello, nets for large-scale fishing.

But Basterra had enough of this product—nobody wanted it. He was accumulating mountains of it in storage, and when he was able to sell the merchandise it was at a fraction of its supposed value. Each head of cocuiza was meant to be worth one real, but he could only sell it for half that amount. Each hammock was expected to sell for eight reales, or one peso, but could only sell for three reales. Given that his district was responsible

---

480 Ibid., 163.

for footing the transportation costs, Puerto Cabello was hemorrhaging money because of Coro's useless tributes.

Venezuela's Governor at the time, Juan de Guillelmi, responded by contacting Coro's treasurer to see if their tributaries could pay with a more useful product. But José de Navarrete rejected the proposal, stating that Coro's Indigenous people did not have anything else to contribute. The treasurer added, "the great poverty of the natives, the miserable situations of their towns, does not allow them to subsist, nor to dress, and much less to provide subsistence for their families."[481] But as a compromise, Navarrete said that from that point forward he would only accept hammocks as payment, and refuse the cocuiza that was used to produce them.[482] Despite this agreement, Puerto Cabello's treasurer eventually got his wish—all shipments of Coro's Indigenous tribute were halted the following year.

But if tribute payments were a burden for royal administrators, they were a millstone for Indigenous people. Hammocks and cocuiza were the most useful and tangible commodities they could produce. But the plant was hard to come by. According to Navarrete, there was a time when cocuiza was accessible, but that time had long passed. Getting it in the late 18th century was a "difficult and drawn-out" process.[483]

Tribute amounts varied from pueblo to pueblo, from one peso a year to four pesos and six reales a year. In San Luis and Pecaya, married men paid two pesos annually, while single men above the age of 18 paid half that. In the place of Chirino's birth, Pedregal, married men paid four pesos and six reales a year, while single men above 18 paid two pesos and six reales.[484]

---

481 "Expediente", ff. 7-8: "la grande pobreza de los naturales, y miseria de las situationes de sus Pueblos, no les brinda conmodo alguno para sustentarse ni vestirse, y mucho menos para conservera la subsistencia de sus familias."
482 Ibid.
483 Ibid.
484 Martí, 78-84.

But tribute payments were just one of the many ways in which Indigenous labor-power was usurped. Indigenous people were also responsible for conducting mandatory military patrols, as well as paying a host of other fees like the alcabala, corregidor allowances, and church dues. Some of these payment amounts were as high as tribute. The Jirajaras, Ajaguas, and Ayamanes were exempt from military service but were required to make all other payments. Although the Caquetío were exempt from tribute and corregidor fees, they were exploited in all the other areas.[485]

The Caquetío made up "voluntary" patrol units during holidays and times of war. Around Christmas time, 18 months before the rebellion, Caquetío men were forced to guard the city of Coro. The year before, the head guardian of Coro's port, La Vela, stated that the Caquetío of Carrizal guarded it during Holy Week, while those of Acurigua protected other locations. The Caquetío from Cumarebo shielded La Vela during times of war. Because the conflict with revolutionary France and Saint-Domingue was running its course, they were keeping watch at the time of the insurrection in order to warn authorities of any incoming boats.[486]

But the most despised institution was probably the alcabala, a sales and transport tax imposed on residents throughout Spain and its colonies. It was first levied in Spain in 1342 in order to raise funds for the Crown's struggle against the Moors.[487] In Venezuela, the tax was first put into effect on August 4, 1596, for a period of nine years. The duty returned from 1624-1630, and in

---

485 The Jirajaras, who were considered the most dangerous, devilish, and unruly Indigenous peoples during the period of the European conquest, appear to have been slaughtered by the Europeans at some point prior to the 18th century, although it is possible that they were incorporated into neighboring Indigenous communities. Caracas's Archbishop Mariano Martí visited the region in 1771 and did not report the existence of Jirajara groups in Coro, although he did recognize the three other groups.

486 "Cumarebo: Autos seguidos contra el Teniente Justicia Mayor de la jurisdiccion de Coro por los maltratos que ha dado a los Indios y la introduccion de negros de Curacao," 1794, Indígenas Tomo VII, AGN, ff. 443-5.

487 Depons, 13.

1652 King Philip IV made it a permanent institution in Venezuela.[488] The alcabala was to be charged at 2% on all transactions, whether they were traded for coin or kind, and the payments could be made in a like fashion.[489] On July 1, 1753, the Governor of Venezuela, Don Phelipe Ricardos, increased the alcabala payment to 5%, and this was the going rate at the time of the insurrection.[490]

But Coro's authorities did not always appreciate the importance of the alcabala, at least not according to Don José de Abalos, who spoke out after taking over as treasurer. The whistleblower claimed that eight months of alcabala payments from the years 1765-1766 were missing from several towns in Coro's region. He insinuated that the fees were embezzled.[491]

Just as concerning, Abalos added that Coro's previous treasurers had utterly failed to collect alcabala on all goods that were transported, purchased, and sold. Using an example, the new treasurer stated that in the previous two years, Coro only collected tax on the sale of 1,500 bovine animals. This was disturbing because 10 times that many were traded during the period in question. Furthermore, Abalos claimed that Coro's treasury did not charge alcabala on corn and cassava, perhaps the two most important dietary items marketed.[492]

Thanks in part to Abalos, alcabala collection soared once Don Francisco de Yturbe took office in 1792. From 1788 to 1791, Coro's treasury averaged an income of over 3,396 pesos a year from the alcabala.[493] In 1792, Yturbe's office collected 8,096 pesos worth—well over twice

---

488 Arcila Farías (1946), 121.
489 Depons, 13.
490 "Ramo de alcabala de tierra: Reparos generales al cargo," Caracas 574, AGI.
491 Ibid.
492 Ibid.
493 "Cuenta de Real Hacienda de Coro, 1788," Caracas 578, diciembre 31, 1788, AGI; "Cuenta de la Real Hacienda de Coro, 1789," Caracas 578, diciembre 31, 1789, AGI; "Libro manual de la Real Caxa del Departamento de Coro," Caracas 579, diciembre 31, 1790, AGI; "Cuenta de la Real Hacienda de Coro, 1791," Caracas 579, diciembre 31, 1791, AGI.

Year	Amount (in pesos and reales)	Percent increase or decrease
1788	3,809 ps 1.5 rls	0
1789	3,452 ps .5 rls	−9.37
1790	2,430 ps 1 rl	−29.6
1791	3,895 ps .5 rls	60.29
1792	8,096 ps 6.5 rls	107.86
1793	9,036 ps 7 rls	11.6
1794	10,939 ps	21
1795	8,908 ps 5.5 rls	−18.57
1796	6,588 ps 5.5 rls	26

Alcabala payments in Coro, 1788-1796

as much as the previous year.[494] This number jumped again to 9,036 pesos in 1793, and ballooned to 10,939 pesos in 1794.[495] Between 1792-1794, Coro's treasury collected nearly three times the amount charged in the previous three years. This would directly lead to the 1795 insurrection.

Coro's revolutionaries called for the abolition of the alcabala as one of their central demands. On June 2, 1795, Don Manuel de Carrera wrote a memorial from his post in Coro's sierra about how indignant the rebels were about the tax, and how much they hated Yturbe. Carrera said that Chirino had ordered the rebels to kill Josef de Tellería because he failed to find a solution to the people's complaints regarding the alcabala. Carrera wrote that, according to the insurgents, they had "suffered" "violations" from the "treasurer Don Juan Manuel de Yturbe and his administrator Luis Barcena."[496] Car-

---

494 "Cuenta de la Real Hacienda de Coro, 1792," Caracas 580, diciembre 31, 1792, AGI.

495 "Cuenta de la Real Hacienda de Coro, 1793," Caracas 580, diciembre 31, 1793, AGI; "Libro Manual de las Reales Caxas del Departamento y Ciudad de Coro," Caracas 581, diciembre 31, 1794, AGI.

496 "Expediente," ff. 109: "tesorero Don Juan Manuel de Yturbe y su administrador Luis Barcena"; "con indiferencia las injustas aflicciones de los pobres."

rera added that the rebels accused Tellería of seeing "with indifference the unjust sorrow of the poor," which led to his murder.[497]

Poor non-whites were targeted by alcabala collectors. As discussed in the introduction, Tellería's widow, Doña María Josefa Rocillo, quoted Chirino as stating, "Tellería did not impede the tax collector of Coro from charging the alcabala with such excess and rigor." He then added "that the whites were in cahoots with the tax collector so that they did not have to pay, and so that all the weight of the contributions fell onto the arms of the poor."[498]

Chirino's assessment was confirmed by Captain Francisco Jacot weeks after the rebellion. The comandante stated that many Caquetío people had complained of being overcharged the alcabala. According to Jacot, people were routinely forced to give up their personal belongings, such as shirts and earrings, if they did not have the specie to pay taxes on the goods they were transporting.[499]

The situation for Indigenous women was particularly precarious given that they were the ones responsible for marketing. Many women worked in their families' conucos and would travel long distances to sell produce. Just six weeks after the rebellion, María Flores, a widow from the Caquetío pueblo of Santa Ana, complained that an alcabala collector had taken 25% of her corn even though the going rate was 5%.[500]

The colonial state depended on taxes such as the alcabala to function, but the genesis and expansion of the tax went hand in hand with that of plantation and hacienda production. In the aftermath of the insurrection, authorities stated that there were 150 plantations and haciendas in the region of Coro. Of these, 95 were dedicated to raising 29,000 head of livestock each year. Authorities also listed just seven cacao plantations.

---

497 Ibid.
498 Ibid., ff. 260-2.
499 Ibid., ff. 135-6.
500 Ibid., ff. 139-40

Although they did not include figures for sugar plantations, it is likely that most of the 48 remaining estates were dedicated to this activity.[501]

But Coro's labor market was not particularly well developed. Most people were not employed full-time but used plantation and hacienda work to supplement their independent subsistence practices. The average plantation employed around 30 enslaved and legally free individuals.[502] Therefore, the region's 150 haciendas employed approximately 4,500 people. This was only 17% of Coro's population.

With 74% of the region being legally free people of African and/or native American descent, the alcabala had the effect of encouraging peasants to work for wages on plantations and haciendas. Paying taxes for transport and marketing cut into small farmers' independent earnings, thus incentivizing day labor. The imposition of the alcabala impeded the ability of people to sell their goods as they had in the past because they were forced to give up *at least* 5% of the produce they transported and sold.

As well as serving as an important source of state income, the alcabala forced people into local labor markets. Referring again to Chirino's comments to Rocillo, the former stated that Coro's tax collector was charging the alcabala "with excess and rigor." The excess that Chirino discusses is in reference to situations such as the one María Flores found herself in, where she was charged 25% for alcabala instead of 5%. The "rigor" Chirino referred to was the implementation of a stricter taxing policy to replace the lax one that predominated prior to Yturbe's takeover.

The alcabala was not the only tax that burdened the poor, however. The Catholic Church also charged duties.

---

501 Ibid., ff. 1-2.
502 Tellería's will reveals that he owned fewer than 40 enslaved people. About 30 of them worked on his two sugar plantations in the sierra, meaning that he employed about 15 enslaved people on each plantation. But the often legally free life partners of Coro's enslaved people would also labor on plantations.

During his inspection of the Coro district, Martí noted the "contributions" that the Indigenous people of the sierra made to corregidores and priests. Only tribute-paying towns in Coro had a corregidor but all of them had a priest. The priest's duties varied from town to town. But in essence, he was to ensure that all children attended church twice a day and were instructed in the Spanish language. The priest was also tasked with ensuring that adults attended church regularly. In some towns this was only on Sundays and holidays, but in others it was daily.[503]

Priests and corregidores came from wealthy families and were paid handsomely by Indigenous workers. In the sierra, one priest served both San Luis and Pecaya, and Indigenous people paid him 60 pesos a year in the former and 90 pesos in the latter.[504] A different priest served Pedregal and he was paid 90 pesos a year in hammocks, which was likely the form of payment in the other two towns.[505] The corregidor of the sierra served all three Ajagua villages and received an annual payment of 4 reales a year from each Indigenous person.

Tribute-payers were not the only Indigenous people responsible for these payments. In Cumarebo, each Caquetío man had to pay two pesos a year toward the purchase of wax, presumably for candles. In addition, the community as a whole had to pay 194 pesos a year to the pueblo's priest. Therefore, a married couple in late 18th-century Cumarebo was responsible for up to 3 pesos a year in Church contributions. This amount of money was worth about 24 days of work a year.[506]

But not all Caquetío were charged this much. The people of Guaybacoa and Carrizal paid one peso a year to their priest.[507] Those in the Peninsula de Paraguaná paid even less. The 1,900 Caquetío in Santa Ana paid their

---

503 Martí, 40-95.
504 Ibid., 79.
505 Ibid., 86.
506 Ibid., 49-51.
507 Ibid., 40.

priest 180 pesos a year, or less than one real each.[508] Those of Moruy paid the same amount.[509] Santa Ana and Moruy paid low fees because they did not receive much interference from the Church. Santa Ana held services only six months out of the year, and Moruy only three.

After the encomienda was abolished in 1721, labor relations transformed in Coro. Indigenous people went from forced labor on plantations and haciendas to "voluntary" work on these same lands. The enactment and expansion of the alcabala—one of the principal targets for Coro's rebels—incentivized waged labor by diminishing the ability of legally free people to provide their own subsistence.

Once alcabala payments skyrocketed in 1792, the rebels found their livelihoods encroached upon, and many took up arms as a result. But not all of those subjected to the alcabala, and other means of labor extraction, rebelled. In fact, most legally free people, including the Indigenous of Coro, fought for the Crown thinking this gave them a better chance to improve their conditions.

Conclusion

The Ajaguas demanded compensation after they assisted the Crown's counterrevolution. On August 3, 1795, a royal official, Gerónimo Tinoco, stated that the people of Pecaya were refusing to pay tribute because they had been promised exemption if they fought against the rebels. Tinoco reported that Yturbe had tried to charge them two months after the insurrection, but they refused. Their authorities told the beleaguered treasurer that they were absolved of these payments. The leaders threatened that if Yturbe came back asking for tribute, they would "rise up."[510] Adding fuel to the fire, Tinoco

---

508 Ibid., 89.
509 Ibid., 108.
510 "Expediente," ff. 209.

reported that the Caquetío stated that if Pecaya revolted, "they would not take up arms against their comrades."[511]

The Ajaguas of the sierra were not the only Indigenous people refusing to pay tribute in the aftermath of the insurrection. In fact, Tinoco was sent to Coro by Venezuela's governor to investigate claims that the Indigenous people close to Río de Tocuyo were also refusing payments. The town's Intendant for the Real Hacienda, Miguel Francisco de Latiegui, notified Caracas that the people of Jácura had been refusing to pay. Authorities also feared that they were encouraging other communities to do the same. Even worse, rumors began circulating that the people of Jácura were planning another uprising.[512]

The root of these troubles began a few weeks before the insurgency. On April 24, 1795, the Administrator of Venezuela's Real Hacienda, Josef del Abad, issued an "*Instrucción*" regarding tribute payments.[513] Abad ruled that all descendants of tribute-payers were responsible for paying the tax. This was a devastating blow to many zambo communities in Coro, who after lifetimes of avoiding the dreaded payments, were now obliged to make them.[514]

Although word of the ruling did not reach the rebels before they took up arms, the decree would still influence the afterlives of the insurrection. Most of the Indigenous people of Jácura were racially classified as zambos. A month after the insurrection, they told authorities that they were never asked to make tribute payments before, and that they would not start. The administrator did not force the issue, as the Crown made it clear that he was to tread lightly.[515] After conducting his investiga-

---

511 Ibid.: "no tomaran ellos las armas contra sus compañeros."
512 Ibid., ff. 215.
513 "Testimonio de la Ynstruccion formada para las matriculas de yndios y auto de su aprovasion por la Junta Superior de R.l Hac.da," Caracas 514, 24 de abril, 1795, AGI.
514 Ibid., ff. 9-10.
515 "Expediente," ff. 215.

tion, Tinoco concluded that Jácura had, indeed, united to refuse tribute payments.

The alcabala was also a recurring issue after the rebellion. On June 13, a wary Jacot warned his superiors in Caracas that Coro's authorities needed to avoid interfering in the lives of Indians, particularly in charging too much for the alcabala. Jacot stated that this can "upset these peoples who are the largest force in this Province."[516] Jacot sent this letter just five days after indicating the same on June 8, pleading with Caracas to grant concessions to the Caquetíos: "let providence dictate what it believes to be conducive to softening the spirits of those upon whose freedom one can only say depend the defense and conservation of that territory, which they prove time and again."[517] He insisted that not only was the Crown's authority dependent on Caquetío cooperation, but that the Caquetío were not happy, and needed to be granted some favors.

As the historically loyal Caquetío and the opportunistically loyal Ajaguas fought to defend the Crown, a few Indigenous people were punished for their crimes against it. On June 3, Ramírez Valderraín dished out penalties to 55 people implicated in the May rebellion, including seven Caquetíos who were sentenced to 10 years of hard labor in Puerto Cabello. The sheriff stated that the Caquetíos had admitted their guilt and "although these are capital punishment criminals, it is not imposed because of the conspiracy that is feared from their comrades who are up in arms in the garrison of the city because of the insurgency."[518]

---

516 Ibid., ff. 139-40: "disgustar a estas gentes que son la mayor fuersa de esta Provincia."

517 Ibid., ff. 137: "que dicte la providencia que estime conducentte a dulcificar el animo de aquellos, de cuya livertad unicamente puede decirse pende la defense y conservacion de ese territorio, la qual cada ves dan nuevas pruebas."

518 Ibid., ff. 65: "aunque reos estos de pena capital no se les impone por la conspiracin que se teme de sus compañeros que estan en guarnicion de la ciudad sobre las armas por el motive de la insurgencia."

While some Caquetío were punished, others were rewarded. On May 29, 1797, Venezuela's Governor Pedro Carbonell handed out financial rewards for exemplary service. "The Indian Captain" from Santa Ana, Pedro Phelipe, was awarded 25 pesos—a staggering amount of money for the time and place, worth about 200 workdays. Carbonell also gave Phelipe's sargent, Juan Andrés Bernal, 12 pesos, and he gave 10 pesos each to 20 soldiers from their same town.[519] These men were given special attention because they were amongst the very first soldiers to defend the city.[520]

The tribute-paying communities of the sierra, and of Jácura, would eventually be granted rewards as well. In 1798, Carbonell ruled that all tribute payers in the Province of Coro would be, from then on, exempt from these fees. Carbonell argued that this immunity would allow them to "know the appreciation that loyalty merits," after these "yndios" "took part in the laudable action of exterminating the enemy."[521] Carbonell added, "if the qualities of those yndios are accredited, they should be permitted to marry white women so that that population, desolate during the day, shall increase."[522]

This license to marry white women was an extraordinary "reward" for the tribute-paying communities of Coro. It was also a reflection of a patriarchal society that commodified women's bodies. White women in particular were considered a symbol of wealth, grace, and beauty—something coveted by many, and expected to be desired by all.

The awards given to Indigenous individuals after the rebellion were the result of these people's struggles against a deadly process of accumulation by dispossession that began three centuries before. The Indigenous people who took up arms did so because they rejected the

---

519 Ibid., ff. 154.
520 Ibid., ff. 351.
521 Ibid., ff. 16-7: "conozcan el aprecio que merece la lealtad"; "concurrieron a la accion laudable de exterminar a el enemigo."
522 Ibid: "que acreditasen su calidad de tales yndios permitirles casarse con blancas para que se aumentase aquella poblacion desolada en el dia."

colonial imposition of the alcabala, tribute, and Church and corregidor fees. They also repudiated their growing need to labor on plantations, their loss of independence, and their lowly place in Coro's hierarchy of race and class.

The conquest also determined the rebels' defeat. In 1531, the Caquetío were granted certain "concessions" for "allowing" the Spanish to settle in Todariquiba. As part of the deal, the Caquetío were expected to serve as a reserve army whenever the Crown needed their support. Colonial authorities relied on the Caquetío to quash the rebellion, as their chances for success seemed bleak without their help. Ironically, then, the process that induced insurrection was the same that prevented its consummation. This dialectic continues.

Conclusion: The Conquest Continues

After Venezuela declared independence from Spain (1811), the country's Black and Brown majority was still colonized by domestic white creole élites. Slavery was not abolished until more than 40 years later (1854). Even after this, people of African and Indigenous descent (the vast majority of the population) continued to toil for white plantation and hacienda owners.

Internal colonization was complemented by imperial domination from abroad—this time by way of the United States of America. Venezuela's liberator, Simón Bolívar, warned of the pending U.S. Empire just months before his death, writing in 1829 that the country seemed "destined by Providence to plague America with miseries in the name of Freedom."[523] And torment the hemisphere it did. As was the case elsewhere in the Americas, the United States effectively underdeveloped Venezuela, dominating the country's political and economic landscape for much of the 20th century.

But resistance to this command was constant, and a major victory was earned when Hugo Chávez Frías was elected President in 1998. His revolutionary government began a radical redistribution of the country's oil wealth, which improved life conditions for the country's population. Educational opportunities drastically widened for the marginalized majority, as did access to healthcare and housing. The Bolivarian Revolution also resisted

---

523 "Letter to Colonel Patrick Campbell, British Chargé d' Affaires: 'Plague America with Miseries,'" in *El Libertador: Writings of Simón Bolívar*, ed. David Bushnell (New York: Oxford University Press, 2003), 172-3.

U.S. domination in the global arena, and supported liberation movements throughout the world, particularly in the Global South.

Nowhere was Venezuela's solidarity stronger than with its closest neighbors, as 21st-century socialism swept the former colonies of Iberia. Decades of failed neoliberal policies, combined with successful labor struggles and new openings for liberal (bourgeois) democratic space, provided the conditions necessary for a legal revolution. Elected governments in Argentina (2003), Brazil (2003), Bolivia (2006), Honduras (2006), Ecuador (2007), Nicaragua (2007), Paraguay (2008), and El Salvador (2009) enacted policies to restructure their dependent political economies through land reforms, nationalizations, and historic investments in education and healthcare.

These governments also aimed to disrupt the United States' dictatorial control over the planet. "Latin" American integration paved the way through the creation of international political and economic blocs such as The Bolivarian Alliance for the Peoples of Our America (2004), The Union of South American Nations (2008), and The Community of Latin American and Caribbean States (2010). Besides countering the Washington-based Organization of American States—what Fidel Castro once aptly described as the "Yankee Ministry of Colonies"—they served to produce cohesion within the Caribbean, Mexico, and Central and South America. This would allow the region more leverage when dealing with the United States. This impulse toward building a multipolar world also influenced the formation of BRICS (2006), an organization comprising some of the largest emerging economies—Brazil, Russia, India, China, South Africa—and which is a major threat to U.S. supremacy on a world scale.

The Bolivarian Revolution's leadership not only threatened U.S. imperial dominion over the globe, but also the fortunes of the moneyed class at home. Economic sabotage was a permanent feature of life in Venezuela during the Chávez years, with importers and venders hoarding goods, particularly around election time.[524] During this period, the U.S. government funneled hundreds of millions of dollars to their obsequious oligarchic allies in the country in order to overthrow the Bolivarian government.[525] After Chávez passed away, this coterie ratcheted up their political, economic and informational campaigns in an effort to ensure the Revolution's demise. An even nastier war was then launched against the government of Chávez's successor, Nicolás Maduro.

Today, Venezuela suffers a brutal blockade that has devastated the country's oil sector, which accounts for 99% of its exports.[526] People have fled the country in droves as the United States embarked on a more belligerent multi-pronged attack against the country. U.S.-operated and -supported military incursions have seemingly become ubiquitous. U.S. support for Juan Guaidó—a politician practically no one had heard of before the United States anointed him President—and their push to force the country's strongest oppositional sectors to boycott elections have left the country at an impasse.

But despite the pressure and the seemingly insurmountable odds, Venezuela has remained firm thanks to two decades of groundwork. The country's dedication to political education is paying dividends, as much of the public knows that U.S. imperial action is at least partially responsible for their current struggles. This is no small feat. And it's a reflection of the inroads that the Bolivarian Revolution has made in snatching hegemony away from neoliberal and neofascist dominion

---

524 Pasqualina Curcio Curcio, *La Mano Visible del Mercado: Guerra Económica en Venezuela* (Caracas: Editorial Nosotros Mismos, 2016).
525 Eva Golinger's work is particularly useful in tracking US intervention in Venezuela. See: Eva Golinger, *The Chávez Code: Cracking US Intervention in Venezuela* (London: Pluto Press, 2006). Also see: Jean-Guy Allard and Eva Golinger, *USAID, NED y CIA: La agresión permanente* (Caracas: Ministerio del Poder Popular para la Comunicación y la Información, 2009).
526 "Venezuela facts and figures," OPEC. https://www.opec.org/opec_web/en/about_us/171.htm. Accessed September 19, 2020.

over media, culture, and education. Just as important, the Revolution's commitment to the country's peasants and workers has allowed it to provide subsistence for these sectors during this time of crisis through programs such as the *Comité Local de Abastecimiento y Producción* (CLAP)—the local committees for food supply and production.

Venezuela's opposition to the 21st century's version of the conquest mirrors the resistance by Coro's 1795 revolutionaries. The region's Black and Indigenous people took aim at slavery, the alcabala, Indigenous tribute, and all other taxes, being fully aware that these were impositions made by local white oligarchs in order to exploit the non-white poor. They were also conscious that these rulers were part of a colonial system that kept them down; that without establishing an independent republic, they would be forever doomed to the lot that they were trying to break away from.

The rebels were able to launch this movement because the conditions were prime for it. An anti-slavery revolution was underway across the circum-Caribbean. Self-liberated Africans in Saint-Domingue (Haiti) were leading and winning the fight against European enslavers and imperialists. Rumors were circulating that slavery had actually been abolished, and that corruption was preventing these promises from coming into fruition. These happenings coincided with the drastic increase in alcabala charges in the years leading to the insurrection. This imposition made subsistence more difficult than ever, and forced legally free Black and Indigenous people away from the lifestyles in which they found refuge.

But these conditions were exploitable because Coro's peasants fundamentally rejected colonialism, white supremacy, chattel slavery, and taxation. These people valued their families and their wellbeing; they esteemed their personal independence—the ability to labor for oneself whenever they could create the space for it. They rejected the gross legal, racial, political and economic inequalities that defined life in Coro, and they repudiated the dehumanizing labor conditions on plantations and haciendas. Without the presence of these foundational beliefs, the influences of rumors and trends would have carried little weight.

The equitable political and economic practices of the rebels' homelands greatly influenced their decision to overthrow slavery, taxes, and colonial rule. Communitarian customs of the peoples indigenous to the Gold Coast, the Loango Coast, and to Coro, shaped their egalitarian ideas. The political and economic practices on the household and community levels were particularly important. Although not absent of hierarchy, families and towns practiced collective husbandry, and the fruits of these labors were equitably shared.

It is important to note that these material foundations are not unique to these three regions of the world. On the contrary, they are the underlying principles for peasant communities across all epochs and geographical spaces.[527] This book suggests that the study of egalitarian ideas in the Americas during the Age of Revolution has been lacking in materialist analysis.[528] Radical ideas regarding equality did not emerge from the air or within the minds of affluent Europeans. They have been with human beings for millennia, and they are rooted in the peasant economies that humanity has practiced for most of its existence.

Peasants in places like Brittany, Devon, and Flanders produced the materials that were consumed in Coro, and that were used to purchase enslaved people in the Gold and Loango Coasts. The intricate way in

---

527 See the classic James C. Scott, *The Moral Economy of the Peasant: Rebellion and Subsistence in Southeast Asia* (New Haven and London: Yale University Press, 1976).

528 There are notable exceptions to this general rule, led by C.L.R James's classic. See C.L.R. James, *The Black Jacobins: Toussaint L'Ouverture and the San Domingo Revolution*, second edition revised (New York: Random House, 1963). Also see: Jean Fouchard, *Haitian Maroons: Liberty or Death* (New York: E.W. Blyden Press, 1981).

which commodities, such as textiles, were manufactured during this period ensured that affluent white élites were practically the only ones in Coro who could purchase continental goods. This fact both created the region's racialized class system and reproduced it. Coro's plantation owners accumulated capital in order to purchase and display items such as European cloth, and they made money by exploiting enslaved and legally free workers of African and/or Indigenous descent. The purchase of European commodities, then, was one side of a coin. The other was plantation and hacienda work.

This coin was a political and economic system centered in Europe, and guided by varied interests that all coalesced around the need to accumulate capital and extend white supremacy. European crowns, merchants, landowners, and speculators—all guided by disparate motivations—built up empires that created places like Coro. Many of these individuals and institutions were rivals of one another, yet they often worked together.

Europe's joint-stock companies were crucial in making this Atlantic complex function. Europe's peasant or feudal economic structure limited the pool of capital available for merchants and imperialists. The joint-stock scheme, then, allowed various actors—led by royal families—to band together. This way, European élites were able to force open markets for the commodities that they trafficked.

But it would be a mistake to label this Atlantic complex capitalism. This was the period of primitive accumulation, the system that gave rise to our current political and economic predicament. During the 18th century, Europe's Atlantic economy was based on the structure of peasant production, rather than capitalist production. Textile workers had access to both their means of subsistence and their means of production. When compared to capitalism, this method was costly and inefficient. More research is needed to confirm, but this study adds more evidence to suggest that the capitalist mode of production may not have taken over Great Britain's industries until the mid-19th century.

Defining and historicizing capitalism is of uppermost importance for understanding both the past and our present. In particular, we stand to learn more about the history of European imperialism. It is important to note that the logic of feudal production and primitive accumulation was to grow through geographic expansion, rather than through innovation, which is crucial in capitalism. This is not to say that these two systems did not, and do not, include both tendencies. But capitalism's production method *forces* it to strive harder to cut costs, and advance technology in order to do so. It will be important to track the development of the capitalist mode of production in European industries and see how it influenced the nature of imperialism and colonialism. If my hypothesis is correct, that capitalism did not take off until the mid-19th century, this roughly coincides with the advent of formal colonialism in Africa and neocolonialism in much of the Americas.

To conclude, we cannot understand ourselves today if we do not have an accurate reading of our history. If capitalist industry developed much later than is generally assumed, the Americas are not as developmentally "behind" as has been supposed. This can also lend some insight into why certain countries in the Global South have been able to "catch up" through nursing their infant industries instead of serving strictly as consumer markets for western commodities. A clearer understanding of the history of capitalism logically leads to a more precise comprehension of economic development. And this can aid the countries of the Global South as they chart paths toward real equality and true independence—the same goals sought by Coro's revolutionaries.

Appendix

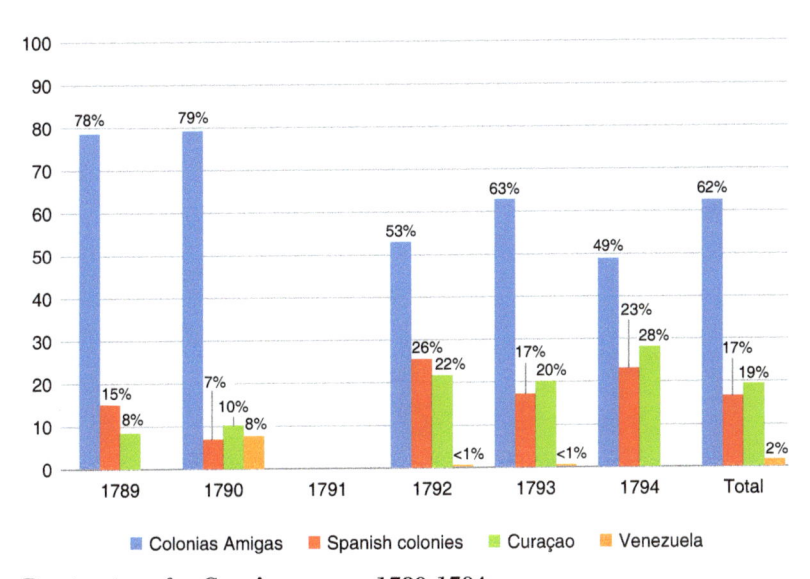

Destinations for Coro's exports, 1789-1794

Bibliography

Archives

Academia Nacional de Historia, Caracas, Venezuela (ANH).

Archivo General de Indias, Seville, Spain (AGI).

Archivo General de la Nación, Caracas, Venezuela (AGN).

Archivo General de Simancas, Simancas, Spain (AGS).

Archivo Histórico del Estado de Falcón, Coro, Venezuela (AHF).

Nationaal Archief, The Hague, The Netherlands (NAN).

The British Library, London, United Kingdom (BL).

The National Archives, Kew, United Kingdom (NAK).

The National Archives-Prerogative Court of Canterbury, Canterbury, United Kingdom (NAC).

Books and Periodicals

"2018 FIU Cuba Poll: How Cuban Americans in Miami View U.S. Policies Towards Cuba." *Steven J. Green School of International and Public Affairs.* https://cri.fiu.edu/research/cuba-poll/2018-fiu-cuba-poll.pdf. Accessed September 4, 2020.

Acosta Saignes, Miguel. *Vida de los esclavos negros en Venezuela.* La Habana: Casa de las Américas, 1978.

Adelaar, Willem F.H. *The Languages of the Andes.* Cambridge: Cambridge University Press, 2004.

Addobbati, Andrea A. "When Proof is Lacking: A Ship Captain's Oath and Commercial Justice in the Second Half of the Seventeenth Century." *Quaderni Storici* 153 (2016): 727-52.

Aizpurua, Ramón. "Revolution and Politics in Venezuela and Curaçao, 1797-1800." In *Curaçao in the Age of Revolutions, 1795-1800*. Edited by Wim Klooster and Gert Oostindie. Leiden: KITLV Press, 2011.

Allard, Jean-Guy and Eva Golinger. *USAID, NED y CIA: La agresión permanente*. Caracas: Ministerio del Poder Popular para la Comunicación y la Información, 2009.

Althusser, Louis. *For Marx*. London and New York: Verso, 2005.

Arcaya, Pedro Manuel. *Historia del estado Falcón*. Caracas: Tip. La Nación, 1953.

Arhin, Kwame. "The Structure of Greater Ashanti (1700-1824)." *The Journal of African History* 8:1 (1967): 65-85.

Arcila Farías, Eduardo. *Economía colonial de Venezuela*. México: Fondo de Cultura Económica, 1946.

Aston, T.H. and C.H.E. Philpin, eds. *The Brenner Debate: Agrarian Class Structure and Economic Development in Pre-Industrial Europe*. Cambridge: Cambridge University Press, 1987.

Beckles, Hilary. *Natural Rebels: A Social History of Enslaved Black Women in Barbados*. New Brunswick, N.J.: Rutgers University Press, 1989.

Borucki, Alex. "Trans-imperial History in the Making of the Slave Trade to Venezuela, 1526-1811." *Itinerario* 36:2 (2012): 29-54.

Boxer, C.R. *The Dutch Seaborne Empire, 1600-1800.* London: Hutchinson, 1965.

Brenner, Robert. "Agrarian Class Structure and Economic Development in Pre-Industrial Europe." *Past and Present.* 70 (1976): 31-75.

------"The Origins of Capitalist Development: A Critique of Neo-Smithian Marxism." *New Left Review.* 104 (1977): 25-92.

------"The Agrarian Roots of European Capitalism." *Past and Present.* 97 (1982): 16-113.

------"Property and Progress: Where Adam Smith Went Wrong." In *Marxist History-Writing in the Twenty-First Century,* edited by Chris Wickham. Oxford: British Academy, 2007.

Brito Figueroa, Federico. *El problema de tierra y esclavos en la historia de Venezuela.* Caracas: Universidad Central de Venezuela, 1985.

Buck-Morss, Susan. *Hegel, Haiti and Universal History.* Pittsburgh: University of Pittsburgh Press, 2009.

Bushnell, David, editor. "Letter to Colonel Patrick Campbell, British Chargé d' Affaires: 'Plague America with Miseries." In *El Libertador: Writings of Simón Bolívar.* New York: Oxford University Press, 2003.

"Cacique Manaure." In Biografias Egly Colina Marín Primera. Eglycolinamarinprimera.glogspot.com/2014/11/cacique-manaure-2.html?m=1.

Campbell, Mavis C. *The Maroons of Jamaica, 1655-1796: A History of Resistance, Collaboration & Betrayal.* Trenton, N.J.: Africa World Press, 1990.

Carneiro, Edison. *O quilombo dos Palmares*. Rio de Janeiro: Editora Civilização Brasileira, 1966.

Carswell, John. *The South Sea Bubble*. Dover, N.H.: Alan Sutton, 1993.

Chapman, Stanley, ed. *The Devon Cloth Industry in the Eighteenth Century: Sun Fire Office Inventories of Merchants' and Manufacturers' Property, 1726-1770*. Exeter: Devon and Cornwall Record Society, 1978.

Childs, Matt. *The 1812 Aponte Rebellion in Cuba and the Struggle Against Atlantic Slavery*. Chapel Hill: University of North Carolina Press, 2006.

Clegg, John T. "Capitalism and Slavery." *Critical Historical Studies*. 2:2 (2015): 281-304.

Coppejans-Desmedt, Hilda. *Bijdrage tot de studie van de gegoede burgerij te Gent in de XVIIIe eeuw: de vorming van een nieuwe social-economische stand ten tijde*. Brussels: Paleis der Academiën, 1952.

Cugoano, Quobna Ottobah. *Thoughts and Sentiments on the Evil of Slavery*. New York: Penguin Books, 1999.

Curcio, Pasqualina. *La mano visible del mercado: Guerra económica en Venezuela*. Caracas: Editorial Nosotros Mismos, 2016.

Dale, Richard. *The First Crash: Lessons from the South Sea Bubble*. Princeton and Oxford: Princeton University Press, 2004.

Davies, K.G. *The Royal African Company*. New York: Octagon Books, 1975.

Davis, Angela Y. *Women, Race & Class*. New York: Vintage Books, 1983.

Dayan, Joan. *Haiti, History, and the Gods.* Berkeley: University of California Press, 1995.

de Amezaga, Vicente. *Hombres de la compañía guipuzcoana, Vol. II.* Bilbao: Editorial la Gran Enciclopedia Vasca.

de Basterra, Ramón. *Los navíos de la ilustración: Una empresa del siglo XVIII.* Madrid: Ediciones Cultura Hispánica, 1970.

de Grandpré, L. *Voyage à la côte occidentale d'Afrique, fait dans les années 1786 et 1787.* Paris, 1801.

Daaku, Kwame Yeboa. *Trade and Politics on the Gold Coast, 1600-1720.* Oxford: The Clarendon Press, 1970.

-----"Aspects of Precolonial Akan Economy." *The International Journal of African Historical Studies* 5:2 (1972): 245.

Defoe, Daniel. "A Tour Through Great Britain (1724)." In *Early Tours in Devon and Cornwall.* Edited by R. Pearse Chope. Devon: David & Charles, 1967.

Depons, F. *Travels in Parts of South America, during the years 1801, 1802, 1803 & 1804, vol. 2.* London: Richard Phillips, 1806.

Duarte, Carlos F. *Historia del traje durante la época colonial venezolana.* Caracas: Armitano, 1984.

Dubois, Laurent. *A Colony of Citizens: Revolution and Slave Emancipation in the French Caribbean, 1787-1804.* Chapel Hill: University of North Carolina Press, 2004.

-----*Avengers of the New World: The Story of the Haitian Revolution.* Cambridge, Mass.: Belknap Press of Harvard University Press, 2004.

Du Bois, W.E.B. *Black Reconstruction in America, 1860-1880.* New York: The Free Press, 1935.

Earle, Rebecca. "Luxury, Clothing and Race in Colonial Spanish America." In *Luxury in the Eighteenth Century: Debates, Desires and Delectable Goods.* Edited by Maxine Berg and Elizabeth Eger. New York: Palgrave, 2003.

Emmer, P.C. "The West India Company, 1621-1791: Dutch or Atlantic?" In *Companies and Trade: Essays on Overseas Trading Companies during the Ancien Régime.* Edited by L. Blussé and F. Gaastra. Leiden: Leiden University Press, 1981.

Estornés Lasa, José. *La Real Compañía Guipuzcoana de navegación de Caracas.* Buenos Aires: Editorial Vasca, 1948.

"Exclusive: Trump cold on Guaidó, would consider meeting Maduro." In *Axios.* Published June 21, 2020. https://www.axios.com/trump-venezuela-guaido-maduro-ea665367-b088-4900-8d73-c8fb50d96845.html

Ferrer, Ada. *Freedom's Mirror: Cuba and Haiti in the Age of Revolution.* New York: Cambridge University Press, 2014.

Fiennes, Celia. "Through England on a Side Saddle." In *Early Tours in Devon and Cornwall.* Edited by R. Pearse Chope. Devon: David & Charles, 1967.

Finch, Aisha. *Rethinking Slave Rebellion in Cuba: La Escalera and the Insurgencies of 1841-1844.* Chapel Hill: The University of North Carolina Press, 2015.

Flynn, J.K. *Asante and Its Neighbors, 1700-1807.* London: Northwestern University Press, 1971.

Fouchard, Jean. *Haitian Maroons: Liberty or Death.* New York: E.W. Blyden Press, 1981.

Fox, Harold S.A. "Outfield Cultivation in Devon and Cornwall: A Reinterpretation. In *Husbandry and Marketing in the South-West, 1500-1800*. Edited by Michael Havinden. Exeter: University of Exeter Press, 1973.

Garate Ojanguren, Montserrat. *La Real Compañía Guipuzcoana de Caracas*. San Sebastián, Spain: Grupo Doctor Camino, 1990.

Garraway, Doris, ed. *Tree of Liberty: Cultural Legacies of the Haitian Revolution in the Atlantic World*. Charlottesville: University of Virginia Press, 2008.

Gaspar, David Barry and David Patrick Geggus, eds. *A Turbulent Time: The French Revolution in the Greater Caribbean*. Bloomington: Indiana University Press, 1997.

Geggus, David Patrick. *Slavery, War, and Revolution: The British Occupation of Saint Domingue, 1793-1798*. Oxford: Clarendon Press, 1982.

-----*Haitian Revolutionary Studies*. Bloomington: Indiana University Press, 2002.

Geggus, David Patrick and Norman Fiering. *The World of the Haitian Revolution*. Bloomington: Indiana University Press, 2009.

Gil Rivas, Pedro A., Luis Dovale Prado and Lidia Lusmila Bello. *La insurrección de los negros de la serranía coriana: 10 de mayo de 1795*. Caracas: Ministerio de Educación, Cultura y Deportes, 2001.

Golinger, Eva. *The Chávez Code: Cracking US Intervention in Venezuela*. London: Pluto Press, 2006.

Goslinga, Cornelis. *The Dutch in the Caribbean and in the Guianas, 1680-1791*. Assen: Van Corcum, 1985.

Hall, Stuart. "Gramsci's Relevance for the Study of Race and Ethnicity." *Journal of Communication Inquiry.* 10:2 (1986), 5-27.

------"The Problem of Ideology—Marxism without Guarantees." *Journal of Communication Inquiry.* 10:2 (1986): 28-44.

Harris, Cheryl I. "Whiteness As Property." *Harvard Law Review.* 106.8 (1993): 1707-1791.

Havinden, Michael, Andre Lespagnol, Jean-Pierre Marchand and Stephen Mennel. "How the Regions became Peripheral: A Complex Long-Term Historical Process." In *Centre and Periphery: Brittany and Cornwall & Devon Compared.* Edited by M.A. Havinden, J. Quéniart, and J. Stanyer. Exeter: University of Exeter Press, 1991.

Havinden, Michael. "The Woollen, Lime, Tanning and Leather-working, and Paper-making Industries, c. 1500-1800." In *Historical Atlas of South-West England.* Edited by Roger Kain and William Ravenhill. Exeter: University of Exeter Press, 1999.

Heijer, Henk. *De geschiedenis van de Wic.* Zutphen: Walburg Pers, 2007.

Hering, J.H. *Beschrijving van het eiland Curaçao.* Amsterdam: S. Emmering, 1969.

Hernández Baño, Adrián. *Los caquetíos de Falcón: Modos de vida.* Coro, Venezuela: Instituto de Cultura del Estado Falcón, 1984.

Hoare, Quintin and Geoffrey Nowell Smit, ed., trans. *Selections from the Prison Notebooks of Antonio Gramsci.* New York: International Publishers, 1971.

Hobsbawm, Eric J. *Age of Revolution, Europe, 1789-1848.* N.Y: Praeger Publishers, 1962.

Hoskins, W.G. *Industry, Trade and People in Exeter, 1688-1800*. Exeter: University of Exeter, 1968.

Hudson, Pat. *The Genesis of Industrial Capital: A Study of the West Riding Wool Textile Industry, c. 1750-1850*. Cambridge and New York: Cambridge University Press, 1986.

Hudson, Peter James. *Bankers and Empire: How Wall Street Colonized the Caribbean*. Chicago: The University of Chicago Press, 2017.

Hussey, Ronald Dennis. *The Caracas Company, 1728-1784: A Study in the History of Spanish Monopolistic Trade*. Cambridge: Harvard University Press, 1934.

Inikori, Joseph E. *Slavery and the Rise of Capitalism*. Mona, Jamaica: Dept. of History, the University of the West Indies, 1993.

-----*Africans and the Industrial Revolution in England: A Study in International Trade and Economic Development*. New York: Cambridge University Press, 2002.

James, C.L.R. *The Black Jacobins: Toussaint L'Ouverture and the San Domingo Revolution*, second edition revised. New York: Random House, 1963.

Klooster, Wim. *Illicit Riches: Dutch Trade in the Caribbean, 1648-1795*. Leiden: KITLV Press, 1998.

-----"Curaçao as a Transit Center to the Spanish Main and the French West Indies." In *Dutch Atlantic Connections, 1680-1800: Linking Empires, Bridging Borders*, ed. Gert J. Oostindie and Jessica V. Roitman. Leiden and Boston: Brill, 2014.

La Rosa Corzo, Gabino. *Runaway Slave Settlements in Cuba: Resistance and Repression*. Chapel Hill and London: The University of North Carolina Press, 2003.

Legassick, Martin and David Hemson. *Foreign Investment and the Reproduction of Racial Capitalism in South Africa.* London: The Anti-Apartheid Movement, 1976.

Levine, David. *Family Formation in an Age of Nascent Capitalism.* New York: Academic Press, 1977.

Locklin, Nancy. *Women's Work and Identity in Eighteenth-Century Brittany.* Burlington, Vt.: Ashgate Pub., 2007.

Lugo, Juan R. and Fulvia M. Polanco, *Reflexiones sobre el zambo José Leonardo y tradiciones de la sierra.* Coro, Edo. Falcón, Venezuela: Editorial Buchivacoa, 1998.

Lynch, John. *Simón Bolívar: A Life.* New Haven and London: Yale University Press, 2006.

Mansur, Jossy M. *E indiannan Caquetío.* Aruba: Imprenta Nacional Arubano, 1981.

Martí, Mariano. *Documentos relativos a su visita pastoral de la Diócesis de Caracas (1771-1784): Providencias.* Caracas: ANH, 1969.

Martin, Phyllis M. *The External Trade of the Loango Coast, 1576-1870: The Effects of Changing Commercial Relations on the Vili Kingdom of Loango.* Oxford: The Clarendon Press, 1972.

Marx, Karl. *Capital, Volume 1.* New York: Penguin Books, 1990.

Martin, Jean. *Toiles de Bretagne: la manufacture de Quintin, Uzel et Loudéac, 1670-1850.* Rennes: Presses Universitaires de Rennes, 1998. https://books.openedition.org/pur/21844.

Mendels, Franklin F. *Industrialization and Population Pressure in Eighteenth-Century Flanders*. New York: Arno Press, 1981.

Mills, Charles W. "Revisionist Ontologies: Theorizing White Supremacy." *Social and Economic Studies* 43: 3 (1994): 105-34.

Mobley, Christina Frances. "The Kongolese Atlantic: Central African Slavery & Culture from Mayombe to Haiti." Ph.D. diss.: Duke University, 2015.

Morgan, Jennifer L. *Laboring Women: Reproduction and Gender in New World Slavery*. Philadelphia: University of Pennsylvania Press, 2004.

-----"Partus Sequitur Ventrem: Law, Race, and Reproduction in Colonial Slavery." *Small Axe* 22.1 (2018): 1-17.

Nesbitt, Nick. *Universal Emancipation: The Haitian Revolution and the Radical Enlightenment*. Charlottesville: University of Virginia Press, 2008.

Palmer, Colin. *Human Cargoes: The British Slave Trade to Spanish America, 1700-1739*. Urbana: University of Illinois Press, 1981.

Paul, Helen. *The South Sea Bubble: An Economic History of its Origins and Consequences*. London and New York: Routledge, 2011.

Perbi, Akosua Adoma. *A History of Indigenous Slavery in Ghana: From the 15th to the 19th Century*. Legon: Sub-Saharan Publishers, 2004.

Pierre, Jemima. *The Predicament of Blackness: Postcolonial Ghana and the Politics of Race*. Chicago and London: The University of Chicago Press, 2013.

Postma, Johannes. *The Dutch in the Atlantic Slave Trade, 1600-1815.* Cambridge and New York: Cambridge University Press, 1990.

Proyart, L'Abbé. *Histoire de Loango, Kakongo, et autres Royaumes d'Afrique.* Paris, 1776.

Rivera, Enrique Salvador. "Whitewashing the Dutch Atlantic." *Social and Economic Studies* 64:1 (2015): 117-132.

Robinson, Casey. *The Fighting Maroons of Jamaica.* Jamaica: William Collins and Sangster, 1969.

Robinson, Cedric. *Black Marxism: The Making of the Black Radical Tradition.* Chapel Hill: University of North Carolina Press, 2000.

Rodney, Walter. *A History of the Upper Guinea Coast: 1545-1800.* New York: Monthly Review Press, 1970.

Rojas, Neruska. "Las criollas y sus trapos: matices de la moda femenina caraqueña durante la segunda mitad del siglo XVIII." In *Se acata pero no se cumple: historia y sociedad en la Provincia de Caracas (siglo XVIII).* Edited by Neller Ramón Ochoa Hernández and Jorge Flores González. Caracas: Academia Nacional de la Historia, 2014.

Rosas González, Otilia. *El tributo indígena en la Provincia de Venezuela.* Caracas: Historiadores SC, 1998.

-----"La población indígena en la Provincia de Venezuela." Ph.D. diss.: Universidad de Salamanca, 2015.

Ruette-Orihuela, Krisna and Cristina Soriano. "Remembering the Slave Rebellion of Coro: Historical Memory and Politics in Venezuela." *Ethnohistory* 63:2 (2016): 327-350.

Rupert, Linda. *Creolization and Contraband: Curaçao in the Early Modern Atlantic World.* Athens, Ga.: University of Georgia Press, 2012.

Sanoja, Mario and Iraida Vargas. *Antiguas formaciones y modos de producción venezolanos.* Caracas: Monte Ávila Editores, 1974.

Schama, Simon. *The Embarrassment of Riches: An Interpretation of Dutch Culture in the Golden Age.* Berkeley and Los Angeles: The University of California Press, 1988.

Scott, David. *Conscripts of Modernity: The Tragedy of Colonial Enlightenment.* Durham, N.C.: Duke University Press, 2004.

Scott, James C. *The Moral Economy of the Peasant: Rebellion and Subsistence in Southeast Asia.* New Haven and London: Yale University Press, 1976.

Sommerdyk, Stacey Jean Muriel. "Trade and the Merchant Community of the Loango Coast in the Eighteenth Century." Ph.D. diss.: University of Hull, 2012.

Sperling, John G. *The South Sea Company: An Historical Essay and Bibliographical Finding List.* Cambridge, Mass.: Harvard Graduate School of Business Administration, 1962.

Stanes, Robin. "Devon Agriculture in the Mid-Eighteenth Century: The Evidence of the Milles Enquires." In *The South-West and the Land.* Edited by Michael Ashley Havinden and Celia M. King. Exeter: University of Exeter, 1969.

Thompson, Alvin O. *Flight to Freedom: African Runaways and Maroons in the Americas.* Jamaica, Barbados, Trinidad and Tobago: University of West Indies Press, 2006.

Vandenbroeke, Christiaan. "Le cas flamand: évolution sociale et comportements démographiques aux XVIIe-XIXe siècles." *Annales* 39:5 (1984): 928.

-----"Proto-industry in Flanders: A Critical Review." In *European Proto-Industrialization*. Edited by Sheilagh C. Ogilvie and Markus Cerman. New York: Cambridge University Press, 1996.

Van der Wee, Herman and Peter D'Haeseleer. "Proto-Industrialization in South-Eastern Flanders: The Mendels Hypothesis and the Rural Linen Industry in the 'Land van Aalst' During the 18th and 19th Centuries." In *Proto-industrialization: Recent Research and New Perspectives in Memory of Franklin Mendels*. Edited by René Leboutte. Geneva: Droz, 1996.

Van Dillen, J.G. "Effectenkoersen aan de Amsterdamsche beurs, 1723-1794." *Economisch-Historisch Jaarboek* 17 (1931): 1-46.

Vasina, Jan. *Paths in the Rainforests, Towards a History of Political Tradition in Equatorial Africa*. London: James Currey, 1990.

"Venezuela facts and figures." OPEC. https://www.opec.org/opec_web/en/about_us/171.htm. Accessed September 19, 2020.

Vološinov, V.N. *Marxism and the Philosophy of Language*. Cambridge, Mass., and London: Harvard University Press, 1973.

Walker, Tamara J. *Exquisite Slaves: Race, Clothing, and Status in Colonial Lima*. New York: Cambridge University Press, 2017.

Wallerstein, Immanuel. *Capitalist Agriculture and the Origins of the European World-Economy in the Sixteenth Century.* New York: Academic Press, 1974.

Wargee of Astrakhan. "The African Travels of Wargee." In *Africa Remembered: Narratives by West Africans from the Era of the Slave Trade.* Edited by Philip D. Curtin. Prospect Heights, Ill.: Waveland Press, 1967.

Wilks, Ivor. *Forests of Gold: Essays on the Akan and the Kingdom of Asante.* Athens: Ohio University Press, 1993.

Yarak, Larry W. *Asante and the Dutch, 1744-1873.* New York: Oxford University Press, 1990.

Youings, Joyce. "The Economic History of Devon, 1300-1700." In *Exeter and its Region.* Edited by Frank Barlow. Exeter: University of Exeter, 1969.

Zoellner, Tom. *Island on Fire: The Revolt That Ended Slavery in the British Empire.* Cambridge, Mass.: Harvard University Press, 2020.